FIRE in her SOUL

Luella Milner Dow

To ████

with many good thoughts

Luella Dow

FIRE in her SOUL

Copyright 1997 by Luella Milner Dow

Published in the United States of America by:
Blue Horizon Publishing Co.
25012 S Harmony Rd.
Cheney, WA ████ 9798

Library of Congress Catalog Card Number: 97-093900

Dow, Milner, Luella,
    Fire In Her Soul

    1. Fiction. 2. Historical Fiction. 3.Washington
Territory. 4. Women's Rights. I. Title

ISBN:0-9658786-0-0

Although this is a work of fiction, Abigail Duniway did, in fact, campaign throughout the Pacific Northwest for a woman's right to vote.

However, any conversation or action in this book attributed to Abigail Duniway occurs only in the author's imagination.

To Wayne,
who always believed.

Special thanks to Christine Tangvald for lighting the spark: to John Bruce for sharing his knowledge of horses and buggys; and to Niki Anderson for her superb editing skills.

Chapter One
THE DECREE

"Wake up, Jake. They're throwing rocks. Jake, Jake! Open your eyes."

The feather tick shifted as Sarah Weatherby dug her fingers into her husband's shoulder.

"Whatsa matter? Quit pokin' me." Jake's voice was thick with sleep.

Sarah leaned over him in the dark. "Somebody's out there. Listen."

As she spoke, pebbles scrabbled over the cabin roof.

"They're throwing rocks, Jake. Can't you hear—"

A sudden splintering sound cut Sarah off. The window exploded. A rock burst through, bounded across the bed quilt and thudded on the rough plank floor. "What's goin' on?" Jake leaped out of bed. "Ouch! Danged glass. Where's my boots?"

Sarah heard him groping as he crunched across the floor. He fumbled for the Winchester hanging from its wall pegs, slipped the safety catch and crept toward the window.

Sarah clenched the quilt around her shoulders. "Who is it? Can you see?"

Jake's white night shirt was a ghostly blur in the shadows. His rifle barrel glinted on the window sill. "Too dark yet. Looks like somebody all hunched over on a horse."

From the lane a raspy voice yelled, "Women's suffrage won't work in these parts, Weatherby. Voting's men's business. Your missus better keep to home where she belongs. Else we'll run her out of Washington Territory."

Another threat. How many had there been? Sarah shuddered.

The advancing dawn showed her the long curve of Jake's back as he scissored his six-foot frame beside the window. He raised the rifle and took aim.

"Gonna give that fellow a dancin' lesson," he muttered.

Sarah flung back the quilt. "No. You mustn't. Let me—"

She rushed to the window. "Wait," she called through the jagged hole. "You don't under—"

Jake jerked her backwards and pushed her onto the bed, pressing his arm across her chest. "Stay down."

She struggled. "You're hurting me."

"Lay still. Better that than have a rock smash you in the face. What have you been up to this time? Somebody's out to get you, Sarah. I told you they would."

Morning broke. She could see Jake's face clearly now. His mouth twisted in anger and his grey eyes snapped.

"Y-yesterday I went to every house on—on Front Street," she stammered. "And I—I asked them to attend next week's meeting with Abigail Duniway." She swallowed. "It means so much to me, Jake. Can't anybody understand?"

Surly tones wafted again through the window. "You been warned, Weatherby."

They heard a muttered "Giddyap." Then the rider's horse galloped away on the hard-packed lane.

Jake released her. "Dad gum it, Sarah. This woman's suffrage thing—it's a fool idea."

"It's not a fool idea. It's only right and proper."

Jake rolled the rock over with the toe of his boot. He frowned at it, then sat on the bed to button his shirt. "Maybe it won't work out here. This isn't Wisconsin. This country isn't settled yet. And anyway, maybe all women won't ever—"

Sarah stood before him in her flannel nightgown, hands on her hips. "Now, just a minute, Jake. Don't tell me you agree with that hide-bound Judge Featherstone. All that talk about women not being smart enough to vote. Jake, don't tell me—"

Jake tugged at her nightgown. A corner of his mouth turned upward. "You give impressive speeches when you're dressed like that."

"Jake—"

"Now, hold off. Just hold off. I never said I agreed with

Featherstone." Jake shrugged into his suspenders. "But he's right on one point, you know. Give women the vote and the next thing you know they'll be runnin' for office."

Sarah's eyebrows shot up. "Well, I don't see what's wrong with that."

"You don't?" Jake picked up the rock and flung the curtain aside that separated the bedroom from the kitchen. His boots scraped across the cabin floor. "I don't suppose you do. By gum, I sure bit off a hunk when I married you."

He jerked the bolt on the cabin door, opened it wide and hurled the rock. Together they watched it pound out of sight into the bushes. The rooftops of Nugget's Front Street, a quarter of a mile away, lined up in silent parade drill. Beyond the town, near the river, loomed the sawmill.

"Smoke's goin' to the ground," Jake said. "Storm's comin'."

Sarah touched his shoulder, let her hand slide down his arm and twined her fingers in his. "I know what I believe is right," she said. "Next year we'll have statehood. Just think of that. We'll be living in Washington State. Wouldn't it be nice if we had women's suffrage along with it? I've dreamed of this so much. I've dreamed and worked and—"

Jake's eyes caressed her face. An inner light flickered in his gaze. "Well then, why don't you just dream about it yourself? Don't try to stir up the whole town."

"You know I can't do that. It'd eat my insides out."

"You still want to keep on? After this?"

She couldn't meet his eyes. He mustn't see the fear that lay just under the surface. "They're only trying to make me quit. You know that."

A worry line creased Jake's brow. His jaw stiffened. "Sarah, maybe a man don't want his wife out sloggin' in the mud, makin' a fool of herself. Can't you just let things be? Don't you know when to stop?" His eyes burned with an emotion she couldn't fathom. "I'll do the chores. You get some grub goin'."

9

Sarah watched him stride down the path, his back ramrod straight and his legs jerking. "He's angry," she muttered. "He thinks I'm making a fool of myself." She leaned against the door frame. "I wish—I wish—" She thumped her fist against the wood. "Why can't he help me? All he wants to do is discourage me."

She closed the door, went into the bedroom and unbuttoned her nightgown. She wadded it into a ball and threw it at the bed.

"Get some grub. That's all men think of. Eating and sleeping. Wives are just property—like horses. I wouldn't be surprised if some husbands even look at their teeth."

Sarah pulled on her ankle-length skirt, wound her long blonde hair into a knot and jabbed the hair pins in place. The broken window glass clinked against the swish of her broom.

"Andy. Andy," she called softly, climbing the ladder to the loft.

Eight-year-old Andy had already crawled out of his bed. He peeked over the ledge.

"Ma, I heard an awful noise and people yellin' and—and—what's that pile of glass on the floor?"

Sarah smiled at her tousle-haird boy. Each day she thanked God for him. The memory of his battle with infantile paralysis would never fade.

She kept her tone casual, "Oh, I guess a bird tried to fly through the window. Now get your britches on before your pa comes in from the barn."

Sarah shoved wood into the cook stove. The fire began to snap. She cut thick slices from a slab of bacon and laid them in the iron skillet.

"I'm going to the spring house, Son. Be sure to put that wedge under your heel when you pull your boots on."

Sarah followed the path around the cabin. Dew-heavy grass dampened the hem of her skirt. She crossed the wooden bridge where channeled spring water gurgled toward the meadow.

Her hand was on the leather strap of the spring house door when she saw the thing.

She gasped and drew her foot back. With quaking knees, she knelt and looked at the object in the path. Someone had laid a crudely fashioned corn-husk doll in the dirt. A hat pin pierced its chest.

"How vicious," she whispered. "Who put this here?"

A part of her wanted to cry and run screaming back to the cabin and bolt the door. Give up, give up, the doll seemed to taunt.

"No," she murmured low in her throat. She set her jaw. Shuddering in disgust, she slowly rose with the doll in her palm. She threw it into a clump of grass and rubbed her hands together as if to erase the imprint of it.

Stumbling a little, she propped the spring house door open with a stick. She stepped inside. Think, she ordered her muddled mind. Concentrate on breakfast.

From a peg driven between the mossy stones she took down a four-pound lard can full of brown eggs. She turned to a shelf on the side wall. "Elderberry," she said on an uneven breath. She ran her finger over the parafined top of the jar and tucked it into the crook of her arm.

A cream crock sat in the swirling rocked-in pool of spring water. Sarah lifted the cloth covering with trembling fingers. "I'd better churn this after breakfast."

After breakfast? Would the world still be here? Would she?

A corner of the cloth had folded upon itself. As Sarah bent to straighten it she heard a twig crack on the path. She looked up. Her heart lurched. A man loomed in the doorway.

CHAPTER TWO
The Deputies

Sarah screamed. The sound filled the spring house, echoing in her ears.

"For the love of—What's got into you, Sarah?" Jake stepped inside and poured a bucket of fresh milk into a crock in the pool.

"It—it's you," she stammered.

"Of course it's me. Who'd you expect?"

She tried a wavery smile. "I—I don't know. Guess I'm just—jumpy. Here." She handed him the bucket of eggs, hoping he wouldn't notice her trembling hands.

They walked single-file to the cabin. Sarah's eyes avoided the grass clump where the doll lay.

"Andy's up," she said over her shoulder as they rounded the corner. Now, if her heart would just settle down and her breath would come back—

"What'd you tell him about the window?"

"I told him a bird tried to fly through it."

"Seems to me he'd better know the truth."

"Jake, he's only a little boy."

"Yeah, I know. You're always remindin' me of that. Only eight years old. Only eight years old. When he's twenty-five are you still gonna say, 'he's only a little boy' as you wipe his nose? When you gonna learn, Sarah, just because he's got a lame leg, he needn't be shielded from the world?"

Sarah's eyes blazed emerald fire. She opened her mouth, then closed it. There was a lump in her throat and tears dammed behind her lashes.

Breakfast was a silent meal. Finally, Jake scraped back his chair. "Takin' the wagon to Three Corners today for supplies. Next week we start surveyin' in that meadow country past Paint Brush Canyon."

Andy jumped up and limped to his father. "Can I go to

Three Corners with you, Pa? Can I go?"

Jake regarded him soberly. "Young man, you have four rows of corn to hoe. Shoulda been done yesterday. Food on the table first, then play. That's a settler's rule, Son. A good one to remember."

Sarah frowned. Jake knew how much Andy loved to go along. Couldn't he relent just this once? She spoke impulsively, "But he could finish the corn when—"

Jake's look stopped her. He stood and put on his hat. "I'll see about gettin' another window while I'm in Three Corners."

He laid a hand on Andy's shoulder and pointed to the pile of broken glass. "Son, old Jed Hathaway brought that window from Fort Walla Walla, jouncin' on the back of a mule. Never even chipped it. Now, in the blink of an eye, it's smashed."

He strode toward the door then looked back at his wife and son. His face softened. "I'll try to bring you both a trinket."

Sarah didn't reply. With her chin lifted and her mouth in a tight line, she was too busy rattling the tin cups in the dishpan.

At that same moment Philip LeCour stood before the mirror in his room over the saloon. He patted his slicked-down hair. Next, he practiced winking at himself. After he had inspected his teeth, he studied the effects of brushing his moustache in various directions.

The dust-cutter he had shared downstairs with Circuit Judge Asa Featherstone simmered pleasantly in his stomach. But his thoughts boiled with excitement.

Free at last. Thanks to the judge. But, as always, when the judge got him out of a scrape there was a price to pay. The judge always saw to that.

They had talked behind the saloon at LeCour's request. "I like to be out in the open air," LeCour had said. "I've had enough of being closed in, not seeing the ground and sky.

What's your next project, Judge?"

LeCour watched Judge Asa Featherstone's greedy pig-eyes glinting as he outlined his plan. "You cozy up to that woman. Get her to trust you so you can manipulate her."

LeCour countered, "What if she don't like me?"

"She will. All women do. You weren't born with those cow-eyes of yours for nothing. I've seen you use them before."

"And what's in it for me?"

"Plenty. If you succeed."

"And if I don't?"

"You will. Work at it until you do. You owe me for springing you out of the hoosegow. Besides, she's dangerous. Women like that could get the whole country riled up. I won't risk letting her spoil my plans for the state house." His eyelids closed to razored slits. "No matter what it takes."

Lecour felt the judge's fat finger pressing hard on his chest, forcing him to step backward.

"You fail and I'll let them keep you locked up next time. Nobody endangers my reputation." Featherstone rocked forward on his toes.

LeCour smelled his sour breath and noted the arrogance in his tone as he continued, "I'm speaking tomorrow at the picnic in Dimlar's Grove. The whole town always turns out. See that you're there."

LeCour had left the judge, climbed the stairs to his room and locked the door. Rubbing his hands together, he chuckled. Somewhere near the pit of his stomach a shiver of anticipation fluttered. Finally, after six years behind bars his chance had come.

He stroked his chin. He'd do the judge's bidding. That part was easy. And he'd do a little extra too. The judge didn't need to know everything. Yes, he'd get even now. "Revenge," he said aloud. "At last."

He flashed a smile. His brown eyes gleamed. He straightened his tie and bowed. "Good afternoon, Mrs. Weatherby," he said to his reflection in the mirror.

While LeCour preened in his room a hunched figure in a threadbare coat lay hidden in the bushes behind the saloon. He waited patiently as Judge Featherstone leaned against a tree and smoked a cigar. Presently the judge gave a slight nod. The hunched man saw the signal and emerged from the bushes. He loitered, scuffing his feet, watching the judge's face.

Featherstone's lips moved. "See that dandy I just talked to?"

The hunched one stooped as if searching the dirt for a lost prize. "Yes, Boss."

"Keep an eye on him. Report to me in the usual way."

The hunched one scanned the ground. "Horses make me sneeze, Boss. I ain't ridin' one again. And I don't like throwin' rocks. It ain't civilized."

He heard the clink of coins in the judge's hand. "You want these? You'll do whatever I say."

The hunched man saw a coin fall to the ground. It raised a tiny puff of dust then settled in the dirt. He heard the other coins jingling as Featherstone strolled away.

In one swift motion the hunched man snatched up the coin and yanked at his baggy pants. He squinted after the judge.

"'Keep an eye on him,' he says. Just like that. How many's he think I can keep my eye on at once?"

CHAPTER THREE
The Diatribe

Sarah heard the jingle of the harnesses as Jake reined the horses in front of the cabin.

"Come on, Sarah," he called through the open door. "We don't want to be the last ones to the picnic."

Sarah smiled to herself and finished pinning her hair. "Heap big husband," she mocked, "Face wilderness with only tripod and transit. Same husband frightened of early-comers at picnic."

She called back, "Give me just one more minute, Jake." She smoothed Andy's collar. "My, don't you look nice."

"Ma, do I have to wear these knickers? All the other boys'll be wearin' overalls."

"But that's because they don't have nice pants like you do." She ushered him out and handed the picnic supplies to Jake.

"I'm the one who ought to be complaining," she said. "Fanny and the mayor are staying home."

"What for?" Jake asked.

Sarah darted a glance at Andy. "You know," she mouthed. "Fanny's close to her lying-in." She looked toward their neighbor's cabin down the rutted road. "And I see Big Lil's out hoeing. She's not coming either. She says the townsfolk make fun of her."

Jake lifted Andy onto the wagon seat. "Can't blame her. It's not easy bein' a half-breed. Not really one thing or the other."

Andy asked, "What's a half-breed?"

Sarah raised her skirt to step into the wagon. "Your pa means that Lil is half Indian and half Irish. Her ma was a Nez Perce Princess. And her pa was an Irish prospector. Lil says he had fiery red—"

"What's a prospector, Ma?"

"A man who searches for gold."

"Did he find some?"

Sarah sat beside Andy and hugged him. "A little, I guess. Now as I was saying—"

Jake clucked to the horses. The wagon wheels creaked. "You ought to get acquainted with somebody besides Lil and the mayor's wife anyway, Sarah." He turned and looked directly into her eyes. "But it might be a good idea if you didn't mention women's suffrage all the time. Some folks don't share your enthusiasm."

Sarah lifted her chin and sniffed.

At the grove Jake unhitched the horses and turned them into Dimlar's pasture. Sarah had wrapped a gooseberry pie in an embroidered dishtowel and held it by the knot. In her other hand she balanced a dish of sweet pickles she had ladled from a crock in the spring house.

"Bring the knives and forks to the tables under the trees, Son," she said over her shoulder to Andy. She untied the dishtowel and folded it under the pie tin. "Now where'd Jake go?"

She spotted him juggling the fried chicken and an old quilt, gesturing as he talked with two overalled farmers. The sharp edge of irritation scraped at her nerves. It was just like Jake to leave her to fend for herself.

A breeze set the pine branches swaying in the grove and played at the blonde curls that framed Sarah's face. She bent her head and compared her pie to the others on the table, her practiced eye noting the thickness of the crusts.

While her attention was on the pies a portly man standing in deep shadow gave a slight nod. A younger man adjusted his cravat. He raised an eyebrow and stepped behind a bush. When Sarah looked up neither man was in view.

Sarah walked over to Jake and took the chicken from under his arm. Andy tugged at her sleeve.

"Ma, Ma, can I go play with some of the boys?"

"Of course you can." Then, as always, she tempered it, "But be careful of your leg."

She looked up just in time to catch Jake's annoyed glance. Their eyes met. His remarks of yesterday washed over her thoughts: '*You gonna wipe his nose when he's twenty-five...?*'

"Sorry," she breathed. "Guess it's a habit."

Jake said nothing. He turned his back.

Sarah sighed and set her chin against the silent rebuke. She noticed a cluster of women beside one of the tables and decided to join them. Her dark blue bengaline skirt swayed as she crossed the grass.

One of the women glanced at her. Sarah smiled and waved. Then she stopped with a jolt. She saw the woman shield her mouth with her hand. Her head wagged toward Sarah. The others leaned close, smirks quivering around their lips.

They were whispering. They were gossiping—about her! Sarah's cheeks burned as if she'd been slapped. Stunned, she turned away. The hurt became an ache that pressed down on her, making her knees weak. She sat on the grass, hearing an occasional irritating note of laughter rise above the muddle of voices.

"Some picnic," she muttered. "My husband can't get away from me fast enough. The women talk about me. I'm some kind of object to be gossiped about, to be laughed at." She leaned over and plucked at the grass, shredding it in her fingers. She gritted her teeth. "I'd like to go over and shake them. How dare they treat me like this?"

Jake's deep voice behind her made her jump. "Sarah? What're you doin' here? It's time to eat. Everybody's dishin' up."

Somehow Sarah endured the picnic lunch, a cardboard smile pasted on her face. Jake finished eating and strolled away to pass judgment on a fellow's new horse.

Sarah glimpsed Andy's blonde head bent over a game of

marbles. She hoped the other boys wouldn't suggest playing tag. Andy couldn't keep up. He might fall...

The town's brass band struck up an off-key rendition of "Clementine". Squealing and puffing, they finished with a flourish that made Sarah wince. A spattering of applause, like wind-blown sheets snapping on the line, swept over the crowd.

Sarah wandered among the trees until she heard a man call out, "Get ready for the program, folks. We got a winner for the keg of nails. It's Doc Barnaby. Give him a hand, everybody."

Sarah sat down with her back to a tree. Jake still had the quilt.

Now a red-faced settler jumped on the platform. While he nervously clenched and unclenched his hands he recited in a sing-song voice his memorized introduction of the speaker.

"...and we are glad that Judge Featherstone lives in our town when he could choose any other town along the river. And mammas, you keep your little ones extry quiet now, so's we can hear the judge."

Sarah shifted her back, adjusting to the tree's rough bark. She watched Featherstone mount the platform. His waistcoat, straining at the button holes, moved in and out as he breathed. She stared at his oil-slicked hair...*second cousin to a wet muskrat...wonder if he feels it dripping down his neck...*

She scanned the crowd for Jake. Surely if she caught his eye...

The settlers stilled. Judge Featherstone cleared his throat. His message sailed over the heads of the people and struck Sarah between the eyes.

"Today I must speak to this assemblage on a matter of grave concern to our families, our communities and indeed, the nation. Into the midst of peaceful villages such as this one have come contentious women as mentioned in the holy book of Proverbs, chapter 27, verse 15. Foolish clamorous women, tearing their sisters from the hearthside, preaching heresy..."

Sarah looked up sharply.

"...even some men, perhaps of deficient intellect, have become mesmerized by the spell of these cunning females with their vicious notions. In particular, there is a certain Mrs. Abigail Duniway who seeks to destroy the husband's rightful place as..."

Sarah said, "Poppycock."

Two or three people near her frowned. A pretty girl of sixteen stared. Sarah ignored them. She watched the judge's flat cheeks and blood-shot eyes.

"...foolish females abandoning their homes..." The judge's face shone with sweat. He sucked in great draughts of air.

"Poppycock," Sarah said again.

"Shhh. Shhh," her neighbors responded.

"...progress in this fair city will be accomplished by men. I say men. Men of reason—who establish order in their own households...who hold tightly the reins...constraining those within their domain who are inclined to mischief and depravity."

Sarah shut him out. Her hands tightened into fists. She read the faces of the crowd and anger flared in her throat.

Husbands nodded approval. Wives seemed awed, even hypnotized by Featherstone's sonorous tones. Here and there a mother hushed a child, then looked up expectantly as if waiting for the next bit of wisdom.

Sarah grasped the fabric of her skirt and crushed the material between her fingers. She longed to jump up, to stamp her foot and shout, "No! No! That's not true!" But she sat rigid, fixing her gaze on the back of a farmer's sweat-stained shirt and waited it out.

At last the crowd rose to applaud. The judge left the platform. Women folded quilts and gathered their children.

Sarah stood up. Snatches of conversation drifted around her. "Some speech, eh? That'll knock the wheels off that women's suffrage band-wagon."

"Yep. Ol' Featherstone sure knows how to tell the truth

plain enough."

"I was about to change my mind. Martha's been after me. But now I think maybe we better leave well-enough alone. No telling what women'll do if they get to thinking they can run things."

"I heard that Weatherby woman was around here somewheres today."

Sarah brushed past them and stood on tiptoe. "Jake, I need you," she muttered through tight lips. "You've got to take me home. I can't stand any more of this."

Pushing and jostling, she marched among the people. Startled by her manner, they stepped aside and followed her with questioning brows.

Suddenly a man blocked her way. She looked up, eyes defiant and ready for battle.

"Good afternoon, Mrs. Weatherby," he said with a voice like cool water.

Chapter Four
The Dandy

Sarah's tone was sharp. "I don't believe I know you. Please let me pass." She snapped her mouth shut on the brittle words, pressing her lips over the cry that begged to escape.

He didn't move. Instead, his eyes searched her face, holding her gaze.

"Your husband asked me to introduce myself. Name's Philip LeCour. Most folks call me Phil."

Anger still smoldered within her. The soothing texture of his voice surprised her, bringing balm to her discordant nerves. She listened through a haze of confusion.

"Jake and I are old friends. We've both seen a lot of rain and shine. Sure is nice to meet you."

*...melted chocolate...His eyes are like melted chocolate...*She felt her shoulder muscles relax, her fists unfurl.

"Are—are you a surveyor too, Mr. LeCour?"

LeCour assumed a jaunty pose. "Well, not just now, ma'am. But I've viewed plenty of uncharted territory."

Sarah found herself repressing an urge to check the buttons on her bodice, although they'd never come undone before. She stepped back a pace. LeCour shortened the distance between them with a quick step of his own.

"Did you enjoy Judge Featherstone's speech, Mrs. Weatherby?"

"Well—er—yes, I—I suppose he—" Oh, why did he have to ask that question?

LeCour's face broke into a devilish grin. "Personally, I think that pompous old politician ought to soak his head in a bucket of tar."

Sarah almost choked. She swallowed, then looked up demurely. "Really, Mr. LeCour? Well, I—ah—have you been away, Mr. LeCour? I haven't seen you before at these picnic gatherings."

LeCour's eyes narrowed. He looked over her shoulder. Sarah glimpsed the momentary sharpness of daggers beneath his brows. The image vanished as he sought her eyes again.

"Seems I've missed a few. But this is my old stomping grounds. And I've come back to—settle some business accounts."

He snapped a twig off a tree branch and shot her an appraising glance. His white teeth gleamed as he leaned forward. "But let's not talk about me. Shucks. I bet you haven't seen the new Kodak."

"Kodak? No, I don't believe I have. What is it?"

"Why, it takes pictures, Mrs. Weatherby, of people, of anything. A fellow named Eastman invented it. He has a factory in Rochester, New York. He's turning them out by the dozens. Now anybody can take snapshots."

Although something in the back of Sarah's mind said 'Caution. Wait', her tongue galloped ahead. "Snapshots? I'm not familiar with that term."

LeCour's gaze roamed her face. "A snapshot is a hunting term, Mrs. Weatherby, referring to the hunter who takes a quick 'snapshot' of his prey."

She could barely breathe. "I see," she said, her mind busy with the double meaning indicated in his eyes.

"Say, I have an idea, Mrs. Weatherby. There's a photographer here in the grove today. He's taking snapshots and demonstrating the Kodak. Why don't we stroll over there while we talk?"

"Well—I—" Sarah hesitated.

"Oh, it's all right, Mrs. Weatherby. You can be at ease with an old friend of your husband." He held out his arm for her to take.

...*calming...like a back rub*...The refrain eddied with embarrassing frequency in her mind.

LeCour led her through the trees. She was keenly aware of his arm beneath the fabric of his sleeve and the nearness of his body.

The photographer stood beside a tripod with a black box perched atop it. A metal case with several black boxes stacked in it sat on the ground beside him.

LeCour stepped forward. "Good afternoon, sir," he said, handing the man a silver dollar. "Would you please demonstrate the Kodak and take a snapshot of the lovely lady?"

Sarah heard herself murmur, "Oh, Mr. LeCour, I'd rather not, I—"

The photographer's handlebar moustache twitched. He looked at the silver dollar, then at Sarah. "Yes, indeed. My pleasure. A lovely subject. Greetings, ma'am." He inclined his head. "If I may?" he inquired as he gently moved her into a patch of sunlight.

Sarah protested again. "But, I—really—I don't think—"

LeCour bent close. "Won't take but a minute. You wouldn't want to disappoint the man, would you?"

Sarah raised her face to LeCour's. "But, I don't—" She let the sentence dangle. She couldn't seem to take her eyes away from his.

"Smile," LeCour whispered.

It was over. Too late, she realized LeCour's face had been close to hers, his hand on her shoulder.

In a daze, she watched LeCour write his name and address on a slip of paper. As if far off, she heard him say, "Send me the finished snapshot."

LeCour guided her to the case of Kodaks. He selected one. "Here. Let me show you how it works," he said. As he placed it in her hands their fingers touched. His were soft, elegant fingers, so different from the callused hands of a Jake Weatherby.

Sarah tried to ignore the shiver of excitement that ran up her arm and struggled to concentrate on his explanation.

"Here's the shutter," he said. "You look through this little hole—"

Brown eyes gleaming, smooth fingers touching hers, soft drawling voice hypnotizing her senses—Surely she'd awaken and discover this was only a dream.

"You know what we can do?" LeCour was saying, "I can teach you to take snapshots and we'll surprise Jake."

"That's very kind—but—Mr. LeCour—I—"

"Phil," he corrected. My name's Phil."

"But, don't you think—that is—Phil—"

LeCour's face wore an impish grin. "There. You called me Phil. And may I call you Sarah? First names—friends. Besides, Kodaking is fun. Give you something to do out here so far away from your kinfolks back East. Jake ought to have thought of that himself. We'll just give him a little surprise. That's what we'll do. What do you say, Sarah?"

"Well, yes, of course, it would be fun to surprise Jake—"

"Then it's settled." He turned slightly, looking past her.

For an instant she glimpsed again the dagger points in his eyes. Then he laughed. There was something intimate in that laugh.

"It's been a real pleasure meeting you, Sarah. I'd better return you to your husband. He must be wondering who captured you. Now, where is—"

Sarah heard herself say, "Oh, that's all right. I was just—strolling."

He touched her arm. "Then I'll say good day to you now." He lowered his voice, his tone conspiratorial, "Remember our little secret. We'll meet again."

Sarah blinked and he was gone.

She turned impulsively and looked in the direction LeCour had stared. All she saw was Jake and some other men playing horseshoes. Puzzled, she wandered beneath the trees.

She rubbed her hands where LeCour's slender fingers had touched hers. A wild violet peeked out among ferns at her feet. She plucked it. A smile tugged at her mouth as she caressed its petals. ...Philip LeCour...*why, he's like an errant breeze that blows wisps of hair in your face then fans out your skirts.*

Frowning into the sunlight, Sarah swayed to a silent

tune. "He said we'll meet again," she murmured. "I wonder..."

The hem of her dress brushed the pant leg of a small hunched man crouched beside a tree. But Sarah was too preoccupied to notice him.

The Weatherbys rode home in the fragrant evening. Andy stretched out in the back of the wagon and dozed with the quilt under his head.

Sarah could not contain her curiosity a moment longer. She flattened her voice, feigning indifference. "Did you ask Philip LeCour to introduce himself to me today?"

Jake snorted and flicked the reins over the horses' backs. "Thought I saw him there. Of course not. No husband in his right mind would ask that rogue to speak to his wife."

Sarah ran her tongue along her teeth. "Is Mr. LeCour a surveyor?"

"Surveyor? Is that what he calls himself? Used to be before they forced him out. He was always scouting out what boundaries he could cross without getting caught. That's what he used to do best. Why all the questions?"

"Just wondering." She kept her eyes averted and hoped Jake wouldn't notice the bright spots on her cheeks. And yet— that devilish smile—those taunting eyes—She shuddered.

"Tired, Sarah?" Jake's roughened, blunt-tipped fingers touched her arm.

Guilt stabbed her. Solid, reliable Jake. A husband any woman would be proud to have.

After a moment, Jake asked, "Did you have a good time at the picnic? Get to know some of the other womenfolk?"

Sarah hesitated. Should she tell him how they treated her? Jake hadn't even noticed. A pang of hurt passed through her chest.

Her eyes blazed in remembrance. "I caught them gossiping about me. I don't mean to complain, Jake, but after all I've done you'd think—"

Jake scratched the back of his neck. "Well, they don't

understand you, that's all. You have to be patient. Give 'em time. Nobody's ruffled the waters before. They're used to their old ways of thinkin'."

Sarah rested her hand lightly on his arm. "I wish you'd been with me during Judge Featherstone's speech. Where were you? I looked and looked and—"

Jake turned his head as if examining the sweet clover that grew rank beside the track. "Let's see—guess I was dickerin' with Neb Hastings for some second-hand lumber about that time. I've heard Featherstone's speeches before. Didn't see any need to—"

Sarah's voice hit a high note. "Didn't see any need? Do you know what he said? He made me so angry. You should have heard him. All that talk about women's place. And quoting from the Bible. That wasn't fair. He twisted it to suit himself. One of you men should have stopped him. Jake, why didn't you? He was so insulting. I wanted to get up myself and—"

"Judge Featherstone's an important person."

"What difference does that make?"

Jake started to laugh until he noticed her expression. "You're serious, aren't you?"

"Of course I am. I don't think half those people knew what he was talking about."

"Probably not."

"He could have said 'I drink hog slop' and they would have nodded and clapped. They just don't seem to—"

"Now, Sarah, simmer down."

"That man's prejudice against women is dangerous. He needs a lesson—"

Jake turned a sober face to her. The laugh lines around his mouth became deep grooves in the fading light. "Believe me, Sarah, Judge Featherstone is not a person to toy with. He can be vengeful. He owns half of Nugget, the lumber mill too. You know that."

"But if somebody doesn't stop him he'll go on spewing

out his poison in every town on his circuit. He's done enough damage already. And it'll get worse. He'll undo everything we've worked for and turn people against us. He called Abigail Duniway a vicious, cunning female. Jake, it was awful, it was -"

A sudden inspiration lit Sarah's eyes. "Maybe Fanny Cantrell would ask her husband to arrange an appointment for me with Judge Featherstone."

Jake's hands tightened on the reins. "The mayor's wife? You don't mean that?"

Sarah nodded. "Yes, I do." Her mind was already busy with plans.

Jake shook his head. "You're walkin' into the jaws of a -"

Sarah wasn't listening. "Yes, Fanny can persuade her husband to do it. That pompous old judge—I'll show him. He can't bluff me. It'll be like David and Goliath, Jake. And just like David, I'll win. You'll see, Jake. You'll see."

Chapter Five
THE LION'S DEN

Fanny Cantrell's dark lashes framed her amber eyes. At twenty-six she had four children and the fifth was due any day.

Sarah viewed her with envy. Fanny looked so maternal in her dimity dress. She had let out the last of the tucks two weeks ago. Now it fell in soft folds over her rounded body.

"Wish it was me 'in the family way' instead of you", Sarah said wistfully. "But Jake just clamps his mouth shut when I mention it might be nice for Andy to have a little brother. Sometimes I think he's afraid that—"

Fanny interrupted. "Afraid? Your husband? He's so strong, Sarah. So self-assured. I can't imagine him being afraid of anything."

Sarah wanted to shout, But you haven't had a child with infantile paralysis. You don't know what it's like to worry if the next one...

Through her musings Sarah heard Fanny chatting on. She dragged her thoughts back into the room and smiled indulgently at her friend.

"... and we're having a girl come to help with the housework. Now that Mr. Cantrell will be getting $100 a month as mayor we can afford a hired girl. I'm so excited about it."

Sarah suppressed a gasp. A hired girl was a luxury she would never even hope to have.

Fannny went on, "I'm all ready for my lying-in. The newspapers are sterilized and we've put Mrs. Steinmetz on notice. She's to come at first sign. And I finished sewing the hem in the baby's christening dress this morning."

She patted Sarah's hand. "There are compensations for you, dear. At least you can get out and about whenever you want. I've been stuck in this house forever, it seems."

Her dark hair, parted in the middle, gleamed in the

sunlight that streamed through the tall windows of her parlor. As the mayor's wife, Fanny lived in a clapboard house in town—no cabin in the country for her.

"All I can do is pull back the curtains and let the sunshine in. And believe me, I do. Every day I stand at the window. I watch the buggies going by and I think, why must I be hidden away until my child is born? Why must I stay out of sight as if I were something shameful?"

She leaned forward awkwardly and poured tea into a china cup for Sarah. "Some day things will change. They're already changing, thanks to you. You're so brave, Sarah. You're envious of my children, but I'm envious of your courage."

Courage? Didn't Fanny know her so-called courage was mostly mule-mindedness and a little bravado thrown in?

She reminded Fanny of the reason for her visit. "You'll speak to your husband then? You'll get him to put in a word for me?"

Fanny set down her teacup. "Of course, Sarah. Mr. Cantrell will be glad to arrange an appointment for you with Judge Featherstone."

Sarah smiled inwardly. Fanny always said 'Mr. Cantrell'. It would be unthinkable to call him Cyrus.

Fanny was still talking. "Although I can't imagine why you would want to speak to the judge." She lowered her voice to a whisper. "Not a word of this to anyone, but I don't see how Mr. Cantrell can stand having the judge wander in and out of council meetings like he does, jingling the coins in his pocket to remind the men they'd better run the town like he wants. Mr. Cantrell says he does that all the time. I know one thing, when women get the vote they'll clean up the political system."

Sarah eyed her friend appraisingly. "Have you asked your husband about his views on women's suffrage? Is he willing to support us?"

Fanny's cheeks grew pink. "You must understand, Sarah, that Mr. Cantrell is in a very delicate position. Very delicate. With Judge Featherstone so close and all. We have discussed it occasionally. Mr. Cantrell's such a dear man. You must remember this is confidential. He tells me privately that he's in favor of women's suffrage. 'Women's enfranchisement', he calls it. Whatever that means. But you understand, he has to be careful publicly. There are so many things to consider. He's doing what he can. When Judge Featherstone isn't around the council members talk together. Secretly, I think they're all with us. But they don't dare to—"

Fanny's excuses began to irritate Sarah. She cut them off. "Would he make a public stand? Have you asked him that?"

Fanny studied the cabbage roses in the carpet. "Well, I haven't really talked to him about it much lately. We've been discussing names for the baby mostly. He likes 'Charles' and 'Florence' while I tend to favor 'Hiram' and 'Esther'. Do you like 'Hiram', Sarah? It has such a—"

Sarah stood up. She felt stifled and bored. Funny, she hadn't noticed before how Fanny rambled. "I'd better run along. Thanks for the tea and the chat. I'm sure next time we meet you'll have your precious little bundle."

Aboard the buggy she lifted the reins and turned Lady into the rutted street. "Fanny's likely to forget everything I asked her," she murmured. "I'd better see the mayor myself."

Three days later Sarah entered Judge Featherstone's reception room. An owl-eyed male secretary ushered her into the judge's dimly lit office. It smelled of leather and dust. Musty volumes lined the walls. Featherstone sat at his desk with his back to the window. Sarah knew this arrangement gave her a silhouette view of the judge and enabled him to observe each flicker of expression on her face.

"Your Honor—", she began. Immediately panic swept her mind free of the words she had so carefully rehearsed.

"Do be seated, Mrs. Weatherby." The judge's tone sounded like someone reminding a forgetful child of his manners.

As Sarah's eyes adjusted to the gloomy room she sensed his probing stare. In her mind she pictured a spider regarding a fly caught in his web.

"Sir," she began again, "do you—do you expect any opposition when the vote is taken to admit Washington Territory to the Union as a state?"

"My, my," he said condescendingly, "You need not fret over matters that do not concern a lady, Mrs. Weatherby. I assure you my colleagues and I expect no trouble." The wattles under his chin wobbled. "I don't mind saying that my influence among my dear friends at the territorial legislature has been considerable in matters pertaining to statehood for this great territory. In fact I may humbly accept the governorship if it should be offered me."

He leaned back in his chair, bringing his rounded stomach into view above the desk top. "News of my administrative talent and my reputation for impartiality and fairness has spread far." His lips stretched in imitation of a smile.

Sarah lowered her eyes in revulsion.

The judge brought his chair to the floor with a thump. A fold of his flabby neck slipped over the edge of his high wing collar. "Now then, my dear." His voice resembled a purr. "Surely the purpose of your visit is not to inquire about a truth already well known." Elbows on the desk, he steepled his fingers and stared at her.

Sarah squeezed her hands together in her lap. She forced herself to smile. "You're quite right, your Honor. I am concerned about a related subject."

Her heart knocked against the fall of brown lace on the front of her dress. "You have wide influence, as you said." She fought to control the waver in her voice. "And I would think you'd want the support of all the citizens if you should become governor."

"Yes. Yes, of course. I should greatly covet their support." He smacked his lips as if he tasted something savory.

Sarah locked her fingers so tightly together that they hurt. "But then, your Honor, how could all the citizens support you when half of them would be denied the right? Half would be disenfranchised."

She had learned the word from Abigail Duniway. It rolled off her tongue none too soon, as her lips began to tremble.

Featherstone's eyes narrowed until they were mere slits in his puffy face. "Disenfranchised? My dear woman, whatever do you mean?"

"I mean, sir, that half the citizens would be disenfranchised because half the population is female. Since we are denied the right to vote we ladies have no power to support or disapprove any matter of state."

She watched red blotches appear on his face and held her feet tightly together to still her shaking knees. "Women, sir. Women have brains, thoughts, opinions, standards of decency, perception..."

She hurriedly spoke the list she had memorized. "...awareness of issues, ability to absorb information, make intelligent decisions—"

His voice exploded, sending vibrations through the room. "Mrs. Weatherby!"

She stopped, her mouth still open.

The floorboards creaked as he rose and lumbered toward her. He bent over until his eyes were even with hers. "I am aware, dear lady," he whispered, "that you have succumbed to the spell of that Duniway woman. I know that your heart goes out to your 'downtrodden sisters'—they who are mere 'slaves to whip-cracking husbands'. Isn't that what she tells you?"

His eyes glittered with malice but his voice contained a syrupy quality, as if the two were detached; voice and eyes belonging to two different persons.

"But you, my dear, are an attractive, intelligent woman. Much too intelligent to be deceived by a female shyster—a blasphemous person who would lead you down a heretical path

33

to shame.

"Do you not remember that women's suffrage has come before the territorial legislature time and time again? And always it meets with defeat. This issue has been passed back and forth like a shuttle cock.

"Don't you realize that women should be above the political process? By some foolish quirk your fair sex gained the right to sport themselves like men at the polls last year. But you lost, proving once again—"

Impulsively, Sarah interrupted. "But that was a rigged case, your Honor. You know that. It was brought by a saloon-keeper's wife. And—"

Featherstone went right on as if she hadn't spoken, "... women's enfranchisement is in direct opposition to the Holy Book—"

She heard herself protesting, her voice strident, "That's not true. I listened to you at the picnic. You twisted the scriptures to suit yourself. You are using your position to broadcast a lie!"

In the sudden silence Sarah heard the ticking of his pocket watch. His eyes never left hers. She stared into them. A distant gong sounded in the back of her mind, echoing Jake's warning: *'That man's not someone to tangle with. I wouldn't risk it...'*

Now Featherstone's hand rested on her shoulder. "My dear lady, I'm willing to forgive this womanly outburst. You have my word that it shall go no further than this room."

Through her dress she felt his fingers pressing into her flesh.

"You are upset, my dear."

She detested the patronizing pressure of his hand, the condescension in his voice. She slid sideways out of the chair as his hand grazed her sleeve on its downward swath.

He repeated, "No further than this room."

Somehow she moved toward the door and held onto the knob for support. She lifted her chin once more. Their eyes met. He stood there working his jaw a time or two before he spoke. The blotches on his face had deepened.

"Those who are unwise," he paused to let his meaning register, "must pay the consequences."

Sarah's own voice traveled a tight wire, "Good afternoon, Judge Featherstone."

The click of her high buttoned shoes echoed in the shadowy hallway as she marched down the steps to the street. She climbed into the buggy. "Home, girl," she whispered to Lady. "Take me home." She urged Lady forward with fingers that struggled to grasp the reins. Pulling away, she glanced up at the judge's window. He scowled at her. The wavy glass distorted his face, giving it a grisly appearance.

Oh, how she wished Jake was home. But he would only say 'I told you so'. She didn't need that kind of comfort. If only there were someone she could confide in, someone who...

She turned into the home lane and saw Philip LeCour coming to meet her.

As she drove up he smiled. "I'll unhitch your buggy, Sarah. Let me give you a hand down."

She had gotten in and out of buggies by herself for years. Why then, did she accept his assistance so eagerly?

LeCour stood close, his voice intimate. "How about giving a poor beggar a cup of tea after he stables your horse?"

Sarah started. She fiddled with her reticule. "Well, I— that is—Jake isn't home, you know and—"

His dark eyes held hers. "Meaning that you shouldn't invite me in? Are you speaking of conventions, Sarah? What are conventions anyway? Something some stuffy old politician like Featherstone might think up. I come to you as a friend. If God hadn't wanted men and women to mingle He'd have built a wall in the middle of the world with the men on one side and the women on the other."

She was still nervous from her meeting with Featherstone. Here LeCour stood, melting her reserve, practically rescuing her from collapse.

A giggle erupted in her throat. His answering laugh sent shivers down her back. Well, why not? She needed someone. It wasn't as if she...

Sarah turned toward the cabin, her skirt flouncing more than she had intended, her voice lilting. "Your tea will be waiting, sir, when the buggy is parked and the horse is stabled."

As her saucy tone echoed in her mind she scolded herself: What else will be waiting? A silly schoolgirl? Or a restrained matron who ought to know better?

And then her guilt doubled. Andy was safely away at Lil's picking berries.

Phil and Sarah idled over cups of tea. In spite of her intentions she found herself revealing the details of her conversation with Featherstone.

LeCour leaned toward her. "He threatened you, Sarah?"

"Yes. I could see contempt in his eyes. It worries me, Phil. I don't know—"

LeCour socked a fist into his palm. "That husband of yours ought to be here taking care of—I won't let Featherstone hurt you, Sarah. Somebody has to look out for you. Anytime you need me, you just tell me. And you go ahead and do anything you want. If you decide to sing a song about women's suffrage in the saloon, that's fine with me and—"

"Oh, Phil. I'd never do that."

"Don't matter what, I'm telling you. You just do it. I'll protect you. You can depend on it."

She half-expected him to throw his arms around her. The thought shocked her. The fierce protectiveness in his eyes shocked her too. She lowered her gaze to her cup. "Thank you, Phil. That means a great deal to me."

Jake had called this man a rogue. Maybe Jake had been mistaken. How could anyone who showed such concern be so bad?

He patted her hand. "I just stopped by to tell you I enjoyed our little chat at the picnic. Now I know I was sent because you needed me."

Mindlessly, she wanted his hand to remain on hers. She knew it was wrong. But he had come when she needed someone. And wasn't she entitled to a little comfort? Jake usually scolded her for her efforts. And it was so lonely, so lonely...

LeCour toyed with his spoon. "I think it would be a good idea if I dropped in once in a while when Jake's not here. Just to make sure you're all right," he emphasized. "Let the gossips waggle their tongues if they haven't anything better to do. That Featherstone's not going to bully you if I can help it. The things he said to you! I don't see how your husband can— Well, I'd better leave that alone."

When he rose from his chair he didn't scrape it against the floor like Jake did. He moved with grace and paused at the door.

"Remember now, if you need anything, anything at all, I'll come. It isn't right. It just isn't right." His eyes seemed to burn into hers. "Goodbye, Sarah."

She stared trancelike at the closed door for several seconds before she picked up the teacups. Phil's hand had cradled this cup. He had sat here beside her...

Oh my! Jake. Jake? She rushed into the empty bedroom and held her hand over her mouth. Try as she might she could not bring Jake's face to mind.

Chapter Six
THE DRIFT FENCE

When Sarah awoke the next morning a kaleidoscope of Judge Featherstone's scowl and the message that hissed from between his teeth twisted in her mind. Then Philip LeCour's face loomed before her. She jumped out of bed and shook her head. She would not think of him.

Sarah hurried through her chores. She tied a clean apron around her slim waist and called Andy. His answer sounded from behind the cabin.

She found him sitting on a stump, whittling a bark-skinned stick of wood. His legs straddled the stump and dangled on either side. His crooked foot turned in.

Sarah swallowed the catch in her throat, watching his sun-spangled hair and his deft fingers skillfully shaping the wood.

Andy held up the stick for her inspection. "See, it's an axe. Like the ones Pa uses." He chopped the air. "Whack. Whack. I'll fall the biggest tree in the woods. I'll make it fall right where I want it. Whack. Whack."

Sarah ran her fingers along the smooth curve of the miniature handle he had fashioned and felt the perfectly formed angle of the blade. "It's just like a real axe, Andy. You've done a good job." She hugged him. "But you mustn't think too much about using a real axe."

"Why not?" He continued chopping the air. "Whack. Whack."

Sarah knelt in the grass. "Because of your leg, Andy. You know—"

"But I'm gonna be a strong man. I'm gonna cut down trees like Pa."

Sarah tried again, "Wouldn't you like to be an artist? You're so good with your hands. And you can draw really fine pictures. Maybe some day you can go to a school for artists and—"

"Whack. Whack. There it goes. Crash. Boom!"

He wasn't listening. He had withdrawn from her. She sighed. "I'm going over to Big Lil's for a little while", she said. "I want you to lead Blossom's calf out to the pasture and tie him where he can eat the tall grass along the fence line. Stay with him and watch that he doesn't get tangled in the rope."

She turned away, then paused. "Be careful getting off that stump. You don't want to fall."

"Aw, Ma."

Sarah sat at the scarred pine table in Big Lil's cabin while Lil poured raspberry shrub into tin cups.

"Made this out of my best berries," Lil said in her deep voice. "I saved it to share when you come to visit."

Sarah let the cool drink trickle down her throat. "Tastes good. The days are certainly getting warmer. You should see the line of farmers outside the smithy, waiting to have their sickles sharpened before haying starts. Last week Jake said he'd have to cut our stand of timothy as soon as he gets home."

Lil sat down. "I was out feeding my chickens the morning Jake left. I saw the Guardian Spirit attend him as he passed through the gap."

"Guardian Spirit?"

"To you, my friend, it would appear as swirling mist. The gap was a deep purple before the sun rose in the sky. A good sign."

Sarah studied Lil's face. In her mind's eye a procession of Indians and Irish prospectors marched through the gap and into the gauzy horizon. "Jake told me how a settler killed your uncle and your brother at the gap. 'Skirmishes', the authorities called it. It was murder, Lil."

"Yes". Lil's eyes clouded with painful memories. "But now the gap is hallowed. Like your Abraham Lincoln said, 'consecrated'. And now the Spirit guards the gap. Those who are kind of heart pass freely. Those who are not—"

"But, Lil. All sorts of people travel the gap. Surely you don't think—"

Lil's eyes glittered. "And haven't you heard of an occasional rock working loose and tumbling down just as someone passes through?"

"But how can you be sure a spirit does it?"

Lil's mouth set in a firm line. "Can you prove otherwise? I say 'the Guardian Spirit'. You say 'the hand of God'. It is the same. Would you agree that God has helpers?"

Why—yes, of course."

Lil's chuckle rumbled in her throat. "Who are we to say what the eternal helpers may do?"

"Helpers—" Sarah said. "That reminds me, Abigail Duniway is holding a meeting at Paisley tomorrow night. Jake expects to be home. And since it's only two miles on the other side of the gap he's promised to take me. Why don't you come with us?"

Lil's face grew somber. "No."

"But, why not? We could take Andy along. He'd like that. And he could sleep in the wagon. You're always having to watch him while I go off somewhere."

Lil folded her big hands on the table. "Those town ladies don't want to see me. They laugh at my hair and my ways. They look at my feet to see if I wear shoes. They think I eat boiled squirrel tails and do incantations to the moon."

Sarah's mouth quirked. "And do you?"

"Only on Fridays," Lil answered with a straight face. "No, Sarah. Folks want me to stay apart. It's more tidy that way. You're my friend. That's enough. You and Jake and Andy."

Sarah leaned back in the rickety chair. During a moment of silence she watched a bunch of dried corn hanging from the rafters twist slowly in the warm air.

Sarah swirled the last of the raspberry shrub in her cup. "I know something of what you've gone through, Lil. You know how much I want to help women gain the right to vote. But instead of cheering me on, they ridicule me. There are men who've even tried to frighten me with threats. Why are they so blind?"

Lil's strong shoulders bulged under her calico dress. "Those who try to frighten someone in his quest to help his fellow man are themselves frightened, Sarah. They shake the fist so you will not see how fearful they are. They put up a drift fence to keep you in your place. I know the drift fence well. If my pa had not owned this land I would be on the reservation with my mother's people."

Sarah said, "Yes. A drift fence, that's what it's like. And Jake doesn't understand. He wants me to give up."

Lil nodded. "Jake fears for you."

Sarah's voice was sharp. "Well, he certainly doesn't show it."

Lil remained calm. "He has talked to me, Sarah."

"And—and what did you say?"

Lil laid her broad hand on the table. "I said, 'Jake, Sarah must do what she must do. It would be wrong to discourage her'."

Sarah said, "Humph. I bet he didn't expect to hear that from you. Believe me, Lil. There are times when I say to myself, why not quit? Nobody cares. But then I think of you. You're my inspiration."

"I'm honored, my friend."

Sarah leaned forward. "I remind myself often, if Lil can endure reproach, I can too."

Lil's glossy black braids swung across her back. "You must follow your dream while you are young. Others will join you if you are right."

"Do you think I'm right?"

Lil didn't answer. She reached for the egg basket hanging from a peg on the wall and motioned for Sarah to follow. They walked the path to the hen house, a saggy-roofed shack, surrounded by a wire enclosure.

"See," Lil whispered. She pointed to a sleek brown hen wriggling through a hole in the fence. Once outside the fence the hen clucked and scratched contentedly in the dirt. A butterfly floated past. The hen cackled and waddled after it. The remaining hens jostled one another and struggled one by one through the hole.

"You understand?" Lil turned to Sarah.

"But you don't want them loose," Sarah protested. "They'll make nests in the grass and you won't find the eggs."

Lil nodded solemnly. "Yes. It's best for me if they stay penned up all their lives and never know freedom." She spread her arms wide. "But see how happy they are now? Every living thing wants freedom—freedom beyond the drift fence."

She stabbed the air with a bony finger. Her eyes were like ebony points of light. "You found your hole in the fence, my friend. Go—go forge your path. And—," she paused for emphasis. "I will entreat the Guardian Spirit to watch over you."

Lil scanned Sarah's face. "I think something else is troubling you. It's hidden in your eyes."

Sarah turned away. "Why—why would you think that?" she stammered. "I'd better get home and see how Andy—"

"Ma! Ma!"

Andy's sharp call startled the two women. He struggled toward them, his face reddened from exertion. "Somebody's watchin' me," he panted. "I saw him. He—"

Alarm knifed through Sarah. "Andy! What are you talking about?"

"He was peekin' at me, Ma. I saw him—"

"Oh, my poor boy. You're so hot. You must have run - "

"I saw him, Ma. He was—"

"Sit down. On this stump. Now then—"

"I'm tellin' you, Ma. He was peekin' through the weeds at me. I was tyin' Blossom's calf to the fence, 'n I turned around and there he was. I ran. I ran hard, Ma. But when I got to where I saw him, he wasn't there. He just—disappeared."

Andy raised his arms in a gesture of bewilderment. "How could he do that so fast, Ma? How could he—"

Sarah passed a hand over her eyes. She didn't answer.

Andy jumped off the stump. "We'd better tell Pa when he gets home. Pa'll—"

"NO!" The word burst from her lips. "No," she said again, more calmly, as Lil and Andy stared at her in astonishment. "We can handle this ourselves. Your Pa has enough to think about."

"But, Ma—"

"I said no, Andy. Now, let's go home."

Lil laid a restraining hand on her arm. "I'll walk with you."

"No, Lil. Thanks all the same. We'll be fine. I'm sure whoever it was is gone by now. Probably some silly boy with nothing else to do but play a trick on Andy."

She turned Andy toward home, aware of the perplexity written on Lil's face.

As they drew near the cabin, Sarah said, "You go on, Son. I'll bring a bucket of water."

She paused at the pump. A breeze sprang up, troubling the bushes and sending a flurry of dust snaking across the path. Suddenly Sarah sensed a presence. A shiver ran down her spine. She whirled around. She saw only the bushes, the heat waves shimmering on the gap's craggy rocks and the timothy hay bowing to the wind.

She took a deep breath and lifted the bucket. "Lil's Guardian Spirit," she mumbled. "Maybe I need one."

A little of the water sloshed on her dress. She started toward the cabin. Engrossed in her thoughts, she did not notice a movement in the weeds. The small hunched man crouching there was close enough to touch her skirts.

Chapter Seven
DUNIWAY'S DISCIPLE

Sarah set the flat-iron on the warming oven lid and inspected her dress. Last year's cream colored bengaline: it would do nicely tonight.

Behind her, she heard Jake's straight-edged razor whissk, whissk, rhythmically against the leather strap hanging from a thong on the wall. He had lathered his face with soap from the china shaving mug and dragged a stool to the wavy looking glass which hung beside the strap.

Sarah smiled to herself at the grotesque expressions Jake made while shaving. She took her dress to the bedroom. Her fingers flew down the row of tiny buttons on her bodice. The dress was snug. Thank goodness nobody in Nugget expected her to wear a whalebone corset. Settler's wives needed freedom of movement for their hard work.

She applied kohl around her eyes. The small silver-gilt looking glass she held in her hand was a farewell present from cousin Amanda in Wisconsin. For her journey West she had packed the looking glass in wool and stuffed it deep into her portmanteau. The bag sat leaning against a pine tree while Jake built their home.

As Jake notched the logs for the cabin walls he would joke with the men helping him, "We might have to give Sarah to the Indians so they'll let us keep the looking glass." The men had laughed at a woman's need for refinements in the wilderness.

Now Sarah laid it down and straightened the fichu on the front of her dress. A breeze stirred at the window. She turned. Jake had removed the jagged remnants of glass from the frame of the window following the rock-throwing episode. "Might as well wait till bad weather to replace it," he reasoned. "Summer's comin'. Won't need it."

Sarah looked toward the gap. Shades of violet and rose wavered as the setting sun cast lances of gold over its jutting rocks. She rested her elbows on the window sill. Would Lil's Guardian Spirit watch over them tonight?

Jake interrupted her reverie. "I hear Lil comin'. I'm goin' out to hitch up the buggy."

Lil's wagon rattled in the lane. Sarah ran to the cabin door. She hugged her friend around the waist and drew her inside by a handful of calico. Lil carried a weather-hardened pine limb with a knot on the end of it.

"You brought a stick?" Sarah whispered.

"Yes," Lil whispered back, "In case I see a snake with a man's face hiding in the weeds."

"Sure you won't go along?"

"You know the answer before you ask," Lil's voice boomed.

Andy clambered down from the loft with a goose feather in his hand. "See what I found, Big Lil? Out by the barn. I saved it for you."

Lil chuckled deep in her chest. "Thank you. And I have a present for you too." From a pocket in the side of her dress she took a speckled egg. She crouched low, meeting Andy's eyes. "This is a special egg for a special boy."

Jake appeared at the door. Behind him Lady jingled her harness, while the lowering sun burnished her coat with copper.

"Evenin', Lil. Good of you to come over and stay with Andy." He observed the stick. "You usin' a cane these days?" He looked past her at Sarah. "Best be on our way."

Sarah noticed the toe of his boot tapping absently on the floor. She saw the frown he tried to hide. She made her voice bright, "Thanks, Lil. Be a good boy, Andy."

Lil grasped her hand and squeezed it. "Go, my friend," she said, her voice like quiet water running deep. "Go where the wind blows you. I'll handle everything here."

Sarah hugged Andy. She and Jake boarded the buggy and turned out of the lane. As she waved goodbye to Andy and

Lil, a wash of sadness flooded over her. Was it a premonition of things to come? She glanced at Jake.

"Look at all the rosehips on the bushes," he said. "Bet we're gonna have a cold winter."

"Yes," she replied, hardly listening. And as they rode toward the gap she couldn't shake off the feeling that fate waited with a thunderclap on the other side.

The meeting was held in an abandoned sheep shearing shed. Flickering kerosene lanterns hung from nails high on the walls. Rough plank benches lined the room. The shearing floor, glossy from the spreading of hundreds of fleeces 'in the grease' still held traces of wool caught in splintery boards. Whiffs of tobacco, home-made soap and sweat mingled with the warm odor of the kerosene.

Sarah pressed forward through the milling people. Jake hung back. Soon they were separated. Sarah sensed the excitement in the crowd. She knew some folks were there to cheer, some to jeer, and there was no way to tell the difference.

A murmur rippled through the crowd. Abigail Duniway appeared on the platform, her height and bulk creating a large shadow on the wall behind her. A stillness settled over the room as if the assembly held a collective breath.

Sarah met Abigail the previous fall just before the rains made the roads impassable. She had waited at the stage station for the mail packet. Abigail walked in. "I want passage on the Concord for a bumpy trip back to Oregon," she had told the ticket agent. Turning to Sarah, she joked, "I get more exercise bouncing around in that tub than I do any other way."

By the time the stage arrived Abigail had recruited Sarah into the women's suffrage movement. "I like to see a young woman with a fiery soul," Abigail told her. "This last tour has taken me all over Washington Territory and I see so many women with no spirit at all. They act as if they've been tied behind the wagon one time too many. Now you, Sarah, can influence this Nugget town if you just keep chipping away.

Don't expect instant results. You won't get them. Perseverance is the key. I'll write to you from time to time and I'll be around again in the spring, Lord willing."

Now Sarah stared appreciatively. Would Abigail remember her? There had been three letters with the infrequent mail packet, each one crammed with enthusiastic advice and encouragement. And between the lines Sarah had sensed determination and the Duniway audacity.

Sarah heard Abigail ask, "May I have that lantern brought nearer?"

Sarah squeezed forward between two fleshy women until she stood directly in front of the platform.

Abigail Duniway looked down and caught Sarah's gaze. She smiled. "Hello again."

She remembers. She knows me. She really knows me. A joyful pulse started at Sarah's throat. She stood on tiptoe and glanced backward, searching the bobbing faces for Jake. She pulled her arm free from the pillowy confines of the closely pressed bodies and motioned for Jake to join her.

"Come up here," she mouthed. But he pretended not to notice. He looked away.

Abigail Duniway began her message on a strong note. "Some of you may be surprised to know that God gave women brains the same as men. Women have a right to be heard, a right to voice their opinions. Though they share equally in the hardships of taming this wild country and assume the yoke of drudgery, they are often regarded as little more than cattle. Generally speaking, their thoughts are presumed to be of no importance in this men's world."

She paused. Lantern light flickered over her face. Some of the men shifted their feet, glancing nervously at their wives.

Abigail continued, "Some men, not all, thank the Lord, are afraid to give their wives the recognition they deserve as free thinking humans. They're afraid that doing so will diminish their own swollen egos."

A booing begun somewhere in the back of the room was

quickly squelched by loud shushing.

"And some men," Abigail went on, "God bless their souls, recognize their wives' intelligence, their wives' contributions to our society and whole-heartedly support their quest for equal suffrage."

Cheers and applause broke forth from the crowd. Directly behind Sarah a man's voice spoke, "So this is what she's up to. Gettin' these folks all worked up. Glad I told Bessie to stay home where she belongs."

Sarah's shoulders stiffened. She turned to identify the man who spoke, but she was too tightly sandwiched between the buxom ladies. Close by, another voice rasped, "Heretic. Heretic. Destroyer of homes. You—"

Sarah glimpsed the vengeful gleam in the man's eyes. He was outshouted by chants of "Hear. Hear." The woman whose ample bosom pinned Sarah's arm to her side said, "Oh dear, I abhor violence. I shouldn't have come. Ernest was right when he said women don't belong in a place like this."

Abigail Duniway's voice carried over the din, silencing the shouters. "Ladies and gentlemen, the battle lines are drawn..."

Excitement built within Sarah. She began to tremble and even felt light-headed. Suppose she fainted? A giggle formed in her throat. Nobody would know the difference. She was so wedged in, she would just be standing there, fainted away. She shook with laughter at the picture of it as she jiggled the flesh on either side.

Abigail Duniway paced the platform. "Who will join our cause? Who will go forth to sow in the fields, helping to reap the harvest of women's rights? Come ladies, come gentlemen, our sisters need you. Come stand with me and be counted on the side of right."

A tall, thin woman with piercing eyes and a sharp-edged nose stepped onto the platform. In her wake walked a man no taller than her shoulder. He kept his embarrassed gaze on the floor. Several women, linking arms, strode across the platform, chins raised defiantly at the crowd. Two men, accompanied by boos and cat-calls, stepped up. One yelled, "I dare you, brothers, to stand up for the ladies. Be a real man."

The pressure on either side of Sarah eased. She looked back once more for Jake. Her emerald eyes shone with eagerness.

He was gone. Gone! Well, she would not wait for him. She gathered her skirts and stepped briskly onto the platform. Abigail Duniway took her hand. "How nice to see you, Sarah."

"You remember my name?"

"Of course. Didn't you get my letters?"

"Why, yes. Yes, I did. But I thought—"

Abigail patted her arm. "I wouldn't forget you, Sarah."

Sarah looked out over the sea of faces. People milled about. The movement, like flowers nodding in a field, made Sarah dizzy. Then she noticed someone small and dark weaving through the crowd. He darted under elbows, squeezed between skirts and advanced through the smoky haze toward the platform. Curious, Sarah watched. She saw him raise his arm.

Something cold and squishy hit her in the face and dribbled down her dress. A woman screamed. Shouts erupted all over the room.

"Stop that man."

"Catch him."

"Grab his coat."

The small hunched figure dodged and twisted just beyond outstretched hands. Two men lunged for him, their fingers raking his coattail. Quickly, he leaped through an open window and disappeared into the night.

"Where'd he go?"

"He's out the window."

"Somebody run after him."

Sarah stared numbly at jostling bodies, flailing arms and sweaty faces. Someone wiped her cheek and brushed at her dress. Abigail Duniway stood towering over her, as if to protect her. Through a trembling blur she heard Abigail's voice. "Are you all right, Sarah?"

Sarah blinked and locked her knees to stop their shaking. "I—guess so. I don't—know—"

It had happened so fast. Who was that small man? Had he purposefully singled her out as the target for his tomato? Visions of the smashed window and the corn-husk doll flashed before her. What would Jake think now? She wanted to scream, to cry. She swallowed instead.

"I'm f-fine," she said in a shaky voice. "No tomato thrower is-is going to stop me."

Abigail Duniway turned back to the crowd. Her voice stilled the tumult. "Ladies and gentlemen, the lady is not hurt. Neither are we deterred. The cause of women's suffrage will go forward."

A chant began in the back of the room and swept toward the front. "Women's suffrage. Women's suffrage. Vote. Vote. Vote. Vote."

Sarah and Jake started home. The full moon silvered the road, changing the appearance of ruts to satin folds.

Jake asked, "What's that on the front of your dress."

"I don't know. Tomato, I guess."

"How'd tomato get there?"

"Somebody threw it."

"At you?"

"No—no, I don't think so. I just happened to be in the way."

"That crowd was packed so tight. Seems kinda funny that you'd be hit directly."

"I—I wasn't in the crowd, Jake."

"Where were you then?"

"I was on the platform."

Jake flicked Lady's back with the reins. "You? On the platform? Last I saw, you were wedged in by two unmovable fence posts down on the floor."

Sarah chanced a nervous giggle. "You went outside,

didn't you?"

"Yeah. Had to stretch my legs. Didn't know the meetin' was about to end or I might have stuck it out and waited for you."

She knew he was making excuses. No use scolding. He hadn't wanted to stay.

"That's when it happened." Sarah's voice took on an eagerness. "Mrs. Duniway called for volunteers to step onto the platform. And I wanted to so badly, Jake. I just had to. I feel so strongly about this suffrage movement. I just—"

"Yeah, I know. You'd bang every male head with an iron rail if you thought it'd do any good."

"—so I got right up on the platform to show my support and then the next thing I knew—something hit me."

Jake remained silent for a few minutes, slowing Lady down for the bumpy ride over the peeled log bridge that led into town.

"Did you see who threw it?"

"No. It happened so fast, I—"

"Did they catch him?"

"No. He just sort of—leaped—right out the window. I never saw anybody move so fast. He was—"

"Is this what you want?" His voice was too calm, too controlled.

Sarah shivered. "What I want? What do you mean?"

"Well, you're so determined to plunge into this thing. You don't know what might happen next. Might be worse next time. You willin' to chance it?"

Sarah hooked her hand into the crook of his elbow. She rested her cheek against his coat. She set her chin. "I'm not going to let this scare me away."

"How much you willin' to take? What if they should go after Andy?"

"Andy? Nobody could be that cruel. They wouldn't dare." She clenched her teeth.

"How do you know they wouldn't? Ever think of it?

Some folks won't stop at anythin'. Guess I'd better lay in a supply of windows. Might need 'em."

Sarah didn't answer. Lady trotted through the sleeping town, past the mercantile store and the livery stable. Sarah swayed against Jake as they turned off the street into the home lane. Big Lil had left a lamp burning in the window. It's glow spilled into the yard. Home. A haven of safety and love. Surely Jake was making mountains out of molehills.

Later, as Sarah lay in bed watching the moon make its eternal journey past the window a coldness started at the nape of her neck and slithered unchecked the length of her body. Andy's breathless cry haunted her: *"He was watchin' me, Ma—peekin' through the weeds."*

She turned her face into the pillow and spoke silently, "I can't turn back. I can't. But, what if they—Dear God, don't let them start in on Andy."

Chapter Eight
THE DALLIANCE

Anton McDougall tallied Sarah's grocery bill on a scrap of brown wrapping paper. "Let's see now, Mrs. Weatherby. Fifty pounds of flour, two bits; two pounds of coffee, thirty cents; one tin of baking powder, twenty-five cents; one package hair pins, five cents; and the two skeins of knitting yarn, four cents. That comes to one dollar and fourteen cents."

The storekeeper unraveled some string from its spindle near the ceiling. The brown twine yielded to his yank with a whirring sound. McDougall wound it around Sarah's packages, twisted it into a knot and broke it with a snap of his wrist.

"There we are. Now if you can handle the parcels, I'll carry the flour to your buggy."

He hoisted the cloth flour sack to his shoulder. As they passed through the doorway the overhead bell tinkled. Lady waited for them at the hitching rail. McDougall upended the sack onto the floorboards of the buggy and slapped flour from his sleeves. "I hope you can carry this into your cabin, Mrs. Weatherby." He backed toward the door of the Mercantile. "I gotta wait on other customers."

Sarah said, "Looks as if you need a boy to—"

The bell tinkled as he disappeared inside.

"—run errands," she finished lamely to herself.

A dray wagon rumbled by. Sarah lifted her skirts slightly to step off the boardwalk.

"Sarah. Let me help you."

LeCour! Sarah's heart skipped, then skipped again as he drew nearer. Before she could collect her emotions he was slipping her packages from her grasp.

"Phil. How nice to see you. But I can manage. Really, I don't mind."

"Of course you mind. Every lady needs a man to help her."

His eyes sought hers and held them. One small package separated their bodies. Phil took it gently from her hand. "Besides, it's a rare privilege to assist someone as pretty as you."

He looked up and down the street. "Where is that husband of yours? He should be—"

Sarah's defenses rose. "Jake's out surveying again. That's his job, Phil. You know that."

LeCour grinned impishly. "How can he stand it, being separated from you for weeks at a time?" He shook his head and clicked his tongue.

"Well, he..." Sarah had no answer for that, at least none LeCour would want to hear.

At the buggy, LeCour said, "Now don't tell me you're going to carry that sack of flour into your cabin over your shoulder."

"Really, Phil, I can manage. Andy and I have a little wagon we—"

"Lucky I came along. I just happen to have some free time." He took her elbow, helped her into the buggy, then stepped in after her.

"I'll drive," he said, seizing the reins from her hands.

"Well, I—do you think you sh—"

"Conventions again, Sarah? I promise not to splash through a puddle."

"But, Phil, this is—"

"This is fun," he interrupted. "Hold on." He urged Lady into a trot, winked at Sarah and began to whistle.

From the corner of her eye Sarah glimpsed two elderly ladies pausing on the boardwalk, their mouths agape as they stared.

The buggy jiggled and swayed past the last house in Nugget. Suddenly they were slowing down and turning into the lane. In front of Sarah's cabin LeCour wrapped the reins around the handbrake.

He turned to her. "You think I'm bold, don't you?"

Sarah gazed at his lips. "Well, maybe a little—"

"No," he said. "A lot. A whole lot. I know it. I embarrassed you, and I'm sorry. But I can't help it. That's the way I am. Besides, those two old ladies probably couldn't tell the difference between Jake and me anyway. Do you see a difference?"

"Oh, Phil, you're being—"

"Come on, what's the difference? Tell me."

Sarah looked away. This maverick of a man, who made her heart skip, who made her blush...She turned back to him. "Philip LeCour, you're outrageous and you know it."

"You're right. I am outrageous. Always have been. Let's get this stuff into your cabin."

After turning Lady into the pasture and putting away Sarah's purchases they lingered at the table. LeCour munched the molasses cookies Sarah set out.

His eyes searched hers. "Judge been bothering you lately?"

"No. I haven't seen him, but..."

"Something else happen, Sarah?"

"It was nothing. I shouldn't worry you with it. I—"

"I'm your friend, remember? I want to know."

"Well, Jake and I went to hear Abigail Duniway. She held a meeting in Paisley. And—and when I stepped onto the platform to show my support—Oh, Phil, she gave such a good speech. If only people weren't so—"

LeCour's hand was on her arm. "What happened, Sarah?"

"I was on the platform and—and—somebody threw a tomato and it—hit me. It was humiliating!"

"You don't know who did it?"

"It happened so fast. I saw a small man, sort of hunched over. He wiggled through the crowd. I saw him raise his hand and—he just jumped through an open window and disappeared. I was shocked. I—"

"Where were all the men in that place? Wish I'd been there. I'd have whipped the fellow. Why didn't Jake do something?"

Sarah stared at the table. She couldn't tell him Jake had gone outside. "He—he was held back by the crowd."

LeCour whispered, "You're a noble woman, Sarah. A brave and courageous woman."

"You think so, Phil?" Her voice sounded high and weak.

LeCour leaned closely, "We're soul mates, Sarah. I knew it the moment I met you. Don't you feel it too?"

She nodded, then wished she hadn't.

LeCour touched her wrist and a tiny charge of electricity quivered there. His voice was husky. "Would you mind if I dropped in sometimes, just once in a while—when Jake's gone—just to make sure you're all right? I'd feel so much easier about you being here alone. I'd consider it an honor. I'm very discreet, Sarah. Only you and I will know."

Sarah nodded. "Yes. Yes, I suppose so," she said in a tiny voice, not daring to meet his eyes. "I do get a little nervous sometimes when Jake's not home, wondering if—"

LeCour sauntered toward the door. "Think of me," he said, his eyes dark and luminous. Then he was gone.

Sarah carried the cookie plate to the cupboard. She forced herself to take deep even breaths. She went into the bedroom, lifted the rug from beside the bed and carried it to the clothesline. With the rug paddle in hand, she beat the rug severely, squeezing her eyes tightly shut.

"Let the image of Phil smiling at me blow away with this dust," she whispered, as if in prayer. "Let it. Please let it. I will not think of him. I will clear my mind of him."

Just as she thought she had conquered her feelings she caught herself grinning while she cleaned turnips for supper.

Chapter Nine
THE DUST DEVIL

Thunderheads billowed on the horizon. The sky turned an ugly yellow. Jake arrived home for a late supper, dusty and hot.

"Looks like we're in for a good one. Sure glad I got the timothy into the hay mow last week."

The family sat at the table. Jake stirred his gravy into the potatoes on his plate. Sarah winced and pressed her lips together as Andy imitated his father. Determined to hide her irritation, she began a conversation.

"Why do you suppose they won't let married women teach?"

Jake looked up, saw her expression and laid down his fork. "I think they don't allow married women to teach because after you have children of your own you get too motherly and don't discipline the little tykes enough. Most school teachers used to be men, you know. Teachers should be stern. Women go around pattin' and sayin' 'now, dear'," Jake made mimicking faces.

Sarah laughed. "Oh, Jake, that's not it and you know it." She sipped her coffee and studied his face. "I believe," she said, "the men who made the rule against married school teachers are the same ones who don't want women to vote."

Jake's face clouded. "Now you're graspin' at straws, Sarah. You know—"

Sarah was not dissuaded. "Yes, I think the two are tied together. It's the men who make the rules and the women who are bound to obey them. We're not—"

"Stop it, Sarah! I didn't come home to listen to one of your tangents."

"—and they make up these silly restraints just to keep us in our place and—"

Jake's chair scraped back. His eyes darkened with

anger. "I'm goin' outside."

His heavy boots clipped the floor as he strode through the open door. He stopped in the pathway.

Andy gulped his milk and lifted his white-mustached face. "What's a tangent, Ma?"

"Well, it's—"

"And what's graspin' at straws?"

Sarah grimaced at the blob of potatoes and gravy mixed together on Andy's plate. "Your pa just thinks I'm making up reasons for things. He thinks I get too upset about..." She looked out the door where Jake stood silhouetted against an amber sky. "...about the way men decide things."

"When I'm a man can I decide things?"

For a moment Sarah said nothing, drinking in Andy's blue eyes and his blonde hair as it gleamed in the lamplight. She sighed. "Yes, Son," she said, turning to speak to Jake's broad back. "I expect you will."

Hours later, in the darkness of midnight the angry clouds released their burden, washing the air and pelting the earth. Lightning tore jagged rents in the sky. Jake murmured in his sleep. Half-awake, he reached to touch Sarah.

"Sorry I got all riled up at supper," he whispered as he pulled her close. Their lips met.

Sarah responded to his kiss. But guilt raked her conscience. It was she who had precipitated their personal storm. Why? Why had she done it?

The next morning at the breakfast table Jake spread butter on his pancakes. "Old man Taggart's hirin' boys to pick rocks out of his field. Payin' two bits a day and dinner. That's good wages. Most folks around here can't afford that. Sarah, why don't you send Andy over there? Give him some experience."

Sarah paused at the griddle, pancake turner in hand. "In this heat? And besides, I don't think his leg would—"

Jake broke in, "Toughen him up a little. Wouldn't hurt

him."

Andy speared a pancake with his wooden-handled fork. "Ma says I can go to see the medicine show today. It's gonna be on Front Street. The man does tricks and everything."

Jake scowled with annoyance. "Tricks, huh? I remember the last medicine show I went to. The man did a trick that pulled the coins out of my pocket right into his."

Andy's eyes were wide with innocent wonder. "Really?"

"What I meant, Andy, was that these medicine men are worse than a carpet-bagger. Now, Son, I let Lady and Moses out to run a little when I was doin' chores. I want Moses to get over some of his friskiness before I go to Three Corners for supplies. You go out after a while and put some oats in the manger then call the horses in. And be sure to shut the corral gate."

"Yes, Pa."

Sarah held the pancake turner in mid-air. "Isn't the corral awfully muddy this morning? Andy's likely to get his boots wet."

Jake gave her a level gaze filled with meaning. "He can do it, Sarah." He drained his coffee cup and Sarah poured more from the blue granite pot.

Jake speared the last pancake and smothered it with butter and elderberry jelly. "You gonna make more of this jelly before the season's over?"

"Of course. Why shouldn't I?"

"Just wonderin's all."

Jake got up from the table. "I'm goin' to the tack room. Got to mend my tripod. Thing's about to break in two. And my transit needs cleanin'. Got some grit in there somehow. That last trip was sure dusty."

He closed the door and Sarah bent over Andy. "Ma'll shut the horses up for you, Son. I don't want you getting your boots wet."

"But, Ma. Pa told me to—"

"Never mind, Andy. I'll do it. Doesn't matter who does

it, just so it gets done."

Sarah fixed him a lunch and packed it in a lard bucket.
"Now have fun at the medicine show."

She stood in the open doorway and watched him limp
down the path. He turned at the gate and waved. Sarah waved
back, clearing away the catch in her throat. "Picking rocks,
indeed," she muttered. "How could Jake even consider such a
thing?"

As Sarah turned inside she saw a Lucifer match lying by
the stoop. Quickly she knelt and scooped it into her apron
pocket. Phil must have dropped it. Had Jake seen it? Would he
wonder how it got there? She heard a steady pounding from the
tack room.

She fingered the match inside her pocket. How'd she
get so tangled up with Phil? It wasn't as if she loved him. "I
don't," she affirmed out loud. "It's just that he makes me feel
special and wants to protect me. And Jake can't think of anything to say but, 'You gonna make more jelly?'"

The more she thought about Phil the more she became
irked at Jake. It wasn't her fault if Phil found her attractive and
wanted to be with her—just to make sure she was safe, she
amended.

Sarah heated water, washed the dishes and poured
dishwater over the gooseberry bush at the corner of the cabin.
Then she carried the cream crock from the spring house and
churned a yellow lump of butter.

She paused for a cool drink, wiping the sweat from her
face. The air was terribly muggy. She gave the butter a final pat
and drained the last drop of whey.

Jake burst into the cabin. His face was red, his eyes
flashing in anger. "The horses are at the end of the meadow.
Can't that boy remember a simple chore?"

Sarah's jaw dropped. "Oh, no! Oh, Jake, I'm sorry, I - "
She started toward him. "It's my fault, I—"

"Your fault?" Jake's voice rose to a shout.

She had to confess. "I told him I'd take care of it. I

didn't want him to get his boots muddy. You know—"

Jake shot her a wild look and ran out the door. Sarah yanked off her apron and ran after him. As she climbed the fence into the field Jake's voice wafted back to her, "...sissy out of him."

The horses stood under a cluster of pine trees near the gap. Their heads were down, their tails slapping at the flies that swarmed over their sweaty backs.

Sarah panted, trying to catch up with Jake. The horses raised their heads. Then with a sudden perverse notion they bolted from the trees. Jake jerked off his hat. He waved and hollered. The horses thundered away, throwing pine needles in his face.

Sarah stood some distance back. Her temples pounded. She heard Jake yelling. The ground vibrated as the horses galloped past her, wafting hot air over her and covering her with dust.

Sarah's world narrowed. She had run beyond the point of fatigue. Her knees moved mechanically. Her legs wobbled. Somewhere ahead through the blur of heat and dirt, two horses ran, always just out of reach.

Sarah made a final lunge, stumbled over a root and fell. Spitting dirt and bleeding from a cut on her chin, she sat up, suddenly aware of a change in the atmosphere.

The horses had stopped once more beneath the cluster of pines. A giant cloud like a huge aluminum lid slowly covered the sky, shutting out the amber glare. The silence was broken only by the whisper of Jake's boots in the dry grass as he edged toward the horses.

"Easy, Moses. That-a-boy. Easy, now. Whoa, Lady." Step by step Jake inched closer to their heaving sides. At last he grabbed their bridles, still soothing them with soft tones.

Birds quieted. Not a branch moved. Then, out of the West came a rushing wind, sweeping and bending everything in its path. Papers, twigs, then boards and branches danced across the ground as if propelled by unseen hands.

"Jake. Help me." The wind tore the words from Sarah's mouth. Her hair wrapped around her face. Her skirts slapped against her legs like live things."

"The storm's awful, Jake. Hurry."

"Hold onto a tree," he yelled back. "I can't leave the horses."

Sarah tilted in the wind, snatched at a tree limb and held on. All around her branches clubbed the air, lashing and striking. Sarah fell to her knees and crawled hand over hand until she reached a pine trunk. She embraced it, gritting her teeth as the bark bit into her cheek."

"Jake! Jake!" she screamed.

Jake struggled with the horses. The wind pushed him backward. He fought to stand upright and gasped for breath.

The horses rolled their eyes. Heads jerking, they stomped and whinnied in fright. Moses stepped on Jake's foot.

"Curses, horse!" Jake yelled. "Get over, durn you."

Finally he pushed between them, his arm muscles bulging as he held their heads close. "Easy, Lady. Whoa, Moses. There, Boy."

Cheek to cheek, the man and his horses stood. The wind raged around them, flattening the grass in snake-like paths. They looked like three friends in a huddle, the wind an unwelcome guest trying to pry them apart.

Sarah squeezed her eyes shut against the swirling dust. She tasted the grit in her mouth. Roaring, surging, screaming, the force of the wind went on and on. Sarah blindly clung to the tree, arms numb, face stinging from flying twigs and dirt.

Then, abruptly, the wind stopped. The trees gave a last sigh as limbs bounced and settled to their natural positions. Sarah raised her head and released her desperate clutch on the tree.

"Jake. Oh, Jake." She stumbled toward him, legs shaking. "Jake".

They were safe. The horses were safe. Her heart welled with emotion. Together they could do anything—tame the wilderness—weather storms...

"Did you pack my grub?" Jake had turned the horses around.

Sarah stared open-mouthed. "Grub?"

"Gotta have some grub. Been delayed so long now, I won't be back till tomorrow." He walked the horses past her and headed for the corral.

Sarah brushed her hair out of her face. An hysterical chuckle began deep in her throat. As she raced to the cabin it grew into wild peals of laughter that echoed over the fields. The horses pricked their ears. Jake cast her a questioning look, never missing a step as he shut the horses in the corral.

"Grub," Sarah said to herself, tears of laughter streaming down her cheeks. "Grub. All he thought about was grub."

She entered the cabin, snatched her apron up and tied it on. She leaned against the kitchen queen, still laughing. "All he thought about was—" Her hand touched the match in her apron pocket. "Oh." The laughter died away. Tears of a different sort traced muddy rivulets down her cheeks.

Chapter Ten
THE DECOY

Andy sat beside the woodbox whittling a piece of kindling. Sarah bent over the kitchen queen. She rolled pie dough while she watched the two chainmen Jake had hired. Their faces reflected dedication as they repeated the oath, "...to execute my duties faithfully and well."

Jake cleared his throat. "Let me show you where we're headed."

The men rolled up their sleeves. Their sinewy arms shone in the lamplight while a circling moth made tiny winged shadows on the table.

Sarah opened the oven door, pulled out fragrant bread and slid in the pies. The kitchen was hot. Jake and his men needed the bread and pies for their trip. She sighed. How long would Jake be gone this time? Ten days? Two weeks?

Jake looked up, his eyebrows raised like question marks. Sarah turned her back and wiped her hands on her apron. She would not let him see how much she dreaded his absence.

She scrubbed the sticky top of the kitchen queen. "Here, Andy," she whispered, handing him a piece of dough she had saved.

Andy rolled the dough between his palms, forming a long strip. Then he dangled it into his open mouth. "See, Ma? I'm eatin' a worm," he giggled.

Jake's voice emerged from the huddle. "There's a stream somewhere in this area to meander. And looks like a swamp here. We'll have to offset that. Probably lots of brush to hack through. Anyway, we won't have to carry iron posts along for monument corners. Ought to be plenty of bearing trees and witness trees we can use."

Sarah slipped out the door and started down the path to the spring house. The sun's last rosy glow had faded to purple.

A breeze made shadows waver in the dusk.

Something more than being left behind bothered Sarah. The secret reason she dreaded Jake's going, the reason she dared not admit to herself, was Phil. The way he looked at her these days and the attraction she felt...Could she trust herself to...

An owl hooted. Sarah jumped. Ever since that early morning when the rock crashed through the bedroom window she dreaded going out after dark. She glanced nervously into the deepening shadows.

In the dimness of the spring house Sarah knelt beside the rocked-in pool and lifted a tin from the icy water. She reached for a mold of butter, turned it onto a saucer and stepped outside.

Her fingers were on the latch when she heard an eerie sound. She held her breath and listened.

"Help. Help." A plaintive call echoed through the trees. "Over here. Help me."

"It's Lil. Something's happened to Lil." Sarah hurriedly set down the butter dish and rushed through the graying twilight.

"I'm coming," she called. "Where are you, Lil?"

"Help. Help." The voice guided her far astray of the spring house.

Then she heard it again. "Help." The cry came from behind her.

Sarah spun around. Fear stabbed her chest, sending prickles along her neck. She saw a piece of paper, pale against the darkening woods, flutter to the ground like a wounded moth. The only sound was the twittering of birds as they settled into their nests for the night. Beyond that, an uncanny quiet hovered in the air.

Somebody had tricked her. Somebody who could mimick Lil's voice. Somebody who wanted her away from the cabin—alone...

She swallowed against the panic rising in her throat. Anger merged with her fear, impelling her to cry out shrilly, "I know you're out here. You—you—hiding from me. You ought to be ashamed of yourself!"

Then, lest her voice break on a sob, she bent and snatched the paper from the dirt. She stuffed it into her apron pocket and forced her trembling legs back to the spring house. Her hands closed around the butter dish. And somehow, somehow, she stumbled toward the cabin.

In the warm glow of the kitchen she set the butter on the table, thankful that Jake and his chainmen did not look up. She opened the oven door to check on the pies. The steamy warmth brought back the color that fear had drained from her face. With jerky movements she sliced thick slabs of the hot bread and served the men.

When only crumbs remained on the plates, Jake scraped back his chair. "Well, fellows, you'll be wantin' to get a good night's sleep. I'll meet you at Jensen's corner about six in the mornin'."

At last the door closed on the chainmen's broad backs. The thumping of their boots on the path died away. Sarah sent Andy up to his loft bed, then puttered around the kitchen.

Jake spoke into the silence. "Somethin' wrong, Sarah?"

She stood with her back to him, stacking plates. "No—of course not."

"I may be gone about ten days this time. Think you can manage?"

"I always do, don't I?"

He crossed the room and turned her around to face him. "Guess what I really mean is, don't do somethin' while I'm gone to get yourself into—What I'm tryin' to say is—Oh, blast it, Sarah. You know what I mean. I don't want to have to worry about you while I'm out there. You're gettin' the town pretty upset with this woman's suffrage business."

Her pride was hurt. He had made her defensive. "What you mean is, I'm like a child that gets into trouble when her pa's not around. Is that what you mean, Jake?"

He struck the table with his fist. "No. You know that's not what I mean. Can't you see what I'm gettin' at? You've got this woman's suffrage thing in your head and—well, there's folks out there who'd like to—just be careful, that's all."

He rubbed his face with a calloused palm. "Sometimes I wish I was a farmer, content to work the land and stay home. Then I'd be close by if somethin'...but surveyin's my life. I can't..."

Her hurt dissolved. She saw Jake's need for assurance. "I know. Don't worry about me. Just go on."

As she spoke, her fingers touched the slip of paper in her apron pocket. She shuddered.

"You cold?" Jake asked, surprised. "It's hot in here. You aren't comin' down with the fever, are you? I heard over at Paisley that half the town's got it."

Sarah shook her head and turned away. She began to wrap the left-over bread in a cloth. "Seems like the air gets chilly when the sun goes down. Fall's coming. Those fellows sure took a hunk of this bread. When it's warm like this it gets eaten so much faster. I'll have to bake more before you know it." Then she shut her mouth, suddenly aware that she was prattling on.

Jake lifted the stove lid and sharpened a pencil with his jackknife over the dwindling fire. "Got to catch up on my field notes before I turn in. Breckenridge's a stickler for details. Got some plat lines to draw too."

Presently Sarah came to stand behind him at the table. She read over his shoulder. "...past a pitch pine, meandered a stream 150 chains, baseline five..." She suppressed a sigh. Jake and his meridians, his chains and baselines. How he loved his work. If he thought she was in danger he might...no, that was unthinkable.

She smoothed the cowlick on top of his head. In an off-handed manner she said, "Guess I'll go to bed."

She lifted a corner of the curtain that served as the doorway into their bedroom and let it fall behind her. There was just enough light penetrating through the fabric for her to read the note.

On an escalating heartbeat she scanned the words: "This is your last warning. Either you cease your women's suffrage activities or there will be calamitous consequences."

Sarah slowly folded and then pressed the note into a tiny square and tucked it under the feather tick. She closed her eyes and mouthed the words. "Calamitous consequences." Strange term for a settler to use. Many of them wouldn't know what those words meant. An educated person penned that note—an educated person who wished her harm.

She listened to her heart thrum a rhythm like a tribal drum beat, warning, warning, echoing through the jungle, beware—beware.

When Jake came to bed she pretended to be asleep. She wanted to cling to him and tell him, don't go. I'm afraid. Instead, she stared into dark spaces and wondered if even at that moment someone was watching the cabin. What would the 'consequences' be when she carried out the next project she was already planning for the suffrage cause?

Chapter Eleven
THE DOCUMENTS

At daybreak Sarah reached across the quilt for the companionable hump of Jake's long body. He wasn't there. Then she remembered. He had left early on the surveying expedition. She was alone—with the note.

She flung back the quilt. Kneeling on cold boards, she dug under the feather tick and pulled out the note. She read its chilling message over and over. Who wrote it? Who was out there waiting and watching?

She needed—oh, she needed someone. Would Phil come today? Somehow, he always knew when Jake wasn't home.

Through the broken window Sarah heard Blossom gently thump the barn door with her nose.

"I'm coming," Sarah mumbled. She hooked her long skirt. Outside, she picked up the scoured and scalded wooden bucket from the bench by the door and trudged to the barn.

Blossom nuzzled her grain, chewing contentedly while Sarah's rhythmic milking filled the bucket. How peaceful, the barn's atmosphere. No threatening notes, no spies in the dark.

Sarah pressed her head against Blossom's flank and heard the rumblings in the cow's stomach. "Blossom," she said, "what am I to do? I can't go around looking over my shoulder for the next brick to fall. Somebody hates me. But who..." The image of flabby cheeks and inscrutable pig-eyes passed through her mind. No, it couldn't be. Not Judge Featherstone. Surely these malicious tricks were beneath the dignity of a judge. No. It couldn't be the judge.

She straightened her shoulders and sighed. Today she had work to do. She must persuade Sam Withers to print some leaflets.

It was Abigail Duniway's idea. In a recent letter she had written, "You must keep on, Sarah. Things are going well in

Oregon. You might try distributing leaflets to spread the word. Keep the fire burning brightly...much affection to you..."

Sarah let Blossom out to the pasture and took the milk bucket to the spring house. At the bench by the cabin door she poured water into a chipped enamel basin and washed her arms and face. She carried the basin to the poplar tree that marked the corner of the yard. As she emptied the water around its base she caught herself thinking, *soon it would be big enough for someone to hide behind...*

The office of Nugget's Weekly News smelled of ink, worn leathers and lubricating oil. When Sarah swept through the door the bell tinkled and Sam Withers ambled from the back room. Wiping his hands on his canvas apron, he said, "Why, Mrs. Weatherby. What a nice surprise. How's the family?"

"Fine, Sam. Thank you."

She laid a neatly-lettered paper on the counter. "I need fifty of these printed, Sam. By Saturday."

Sam glanced at the writing. His face paled. "I-I don't know, Mrs. Weatherby. I've been here ten years now. Never had any trouble. This is—I hear that Duniway woman holds meetings behind saloons. Churches won't let her in. No reflection on you, of course, but—"

Sarah reached into her reticule for a fifty-cent piece and held it for Sam to see.

Sam stopped mid-sentence and stared at the money.

Sarah leaned toward him and made him look her in the eye. "Sam," she whispered, "wouldn't your wife like to vote?"

"Well, she—" Sam looked furtively to each side, although there was no one else in the shop.

"Promise you won't tell, Mrs. Weatherby?"

"You can trust me, Sam."

"Fact is, she'd like to join your group."

"Then, why doesn't she?"

Sam looked at the floor and crumpled his apron nervously.

"Because—because I can't let her. Judge Featherstone

runs big ads in the paper every time there's an election. He never spares the expense when there's a man he supports."

Sarah felt gall rise in her throat. "A man he supports? You mean a man he's got his claws into. Isn't that it, Sam?"

"Now, don't get me wrong, Mrs. Weatherby. I gotta provide for my family same as anybody else. And I try to do what's right. Judge Featherstone says there's a new fella wanting to move in and set up a print shop over by Murphy's Saloon. If Featherstone ever found out I—"

He scratched his bald head, leaving an ink stain on his scalp. "I can't afford to lose the business. Please understand, won't you?"

Sarah thought she had never seen a more pitiful expression. Where was the fiery editor of the frontier, eager to expose the truth?

She masked her disgust and laid a second coin on the counter. Sam cleared his throat. His eyes narrowed. "Guess I could make an exception now and then." He glanced around and whispered, "I could do it on my Blower after I close up."

"Blower?"

"That's my new linotype." He gestured behind him. "Slick little rig, isn't it?"

Sarah looked at the huge machine towering above him. 'Slick little rig' didn't quite describe it.

Pride sparked in Sam's eyes. "Man named Mergenthaler invented it. It even justifies the lines."

"Justifies?"

"You bet. That means it makes the margins come out even all by itself."

"That machine must have cost you a fortune, Sam. And having it shipped all the way out here—"

"To tell the truth, Mrs. Weatherby. Judge Featherstone paid a lot of it. Said it'd be right useful when he wanted me to get some news out fast."

Indignation stuck in Sarah's throat. News, indeed. Propaganda was the word. She eyed the two coins that Sam now fingered. "Saturday," she said.

"Saturday", he nodded. "Before noon—er, Mrs. Weatherby?"

"Yes, Sam?"

"No need to tell where you had 'em printed is there?"

"No, Sam. No need."

Chapter Twelve
THE DOG-WATCH

Andy had been asleep in the loft since nine o'clock. Sarah blew out the lamp. She sat beside the dying fire, waiting. At midnight she lifted her cloak from its hook, tucked a flat package under its folds and stepped outside. The latch clicked softly.

The fingers of the wind raked the moon with clouds. She could barely see. Something scurried across her path and she waited for the flutter of panic in her chest to die down.

Out of the yard and across the track, she fumbled for the old post marking the abandoned trail that meandered behind the town. Her hand touched the weathered wood. She felt with her foot, then carefully climbed down an incline to the overgrown road bed.

Tall bushes and trees blocked the moonlight. An owl hooted. Matted grass tangled around her shoes.

Beyond the bushes to her right lay the backyards of Nugget. Dark rectangular shapes of houses profiled against the satin sky. Sarah named them silently as she passed, "Gramercys', Harbisons', Widow Moores'. She has a big dog. I never thought of that. Please, please, don't let a dog bark."

A rush of wind caused the branches behind her to creak and sigh. Sarah lurched forward. She cried out. Now she'd done it. Half the town would come with suspicious faces and lanterns held high to find who was out here. Standing still, she waited. A dog barked twice...

Almost there. One hundred feet, fifty feet...Near the church the clouds shifted. In the burial yard the moon's silvery light outlined white lambs and doves resting atop high narrow tombstones. The ponderous markers of the wealthy Hutchins family stood like a row of sturdy soldiers on sentry duty.

Sarah crouched beside the fence. The church's two front windows on either side of the door seemed to stare at her reproachfully. The bar across the door resembled a disapproving mouth. She half-expected the bell in the steeple to toll, alerting the town to her stealthy business.

Bending over, shielded by the fence Sarah scrambled toward the gate. It's hinges complained loudly as she slipped in, then dove for the shadowy shelter of bushes beside the steps.

With fumbling fingers she unwrapped her package and slid the contents under a bush. Just for good measure she felt for a rock and placed it on top. There now, fifty leaflets from Sam Withers print shop safely hidden. She could go home.

She pressed the folded wrapping paper into a deep pocket of her cloak and straightened her knees.

The gate hinges creaked. Footsteps. They were coming up the boardwalk straight for the church. She saw shadows. Two shadows blended into one. She heard voices murmuring and feminine giggles. Lovers. That's who it was. Lovers. She sighed with relief.

But a new peril emerged. The lovers strolled the boardwalk, mounted the church steps and stood by the door inches from her head.

Sarah crowded into the branches of the bush. Her movement made a twig crackle. She stood there, head bowed, eyes squeezed shut, listening to their endearments and envisioning their embraces.

Finally the couple descended the steps arm in arm and started down the boardwalk toward the gate, until the young woman had a naughty idea.

She laughed giddily and darted away. "Come and catch me," she teased as she ran toward Sarah's bush.

Sarah cowered, unable to do anything but stare as the girl came closer. Just inches away the girl stumbled and fell to her knees. The young man bounded through the grass and caught her around the waist.

The girl saw Sarah first, her eyes traveling from the long dark folds of her cloak up to the whitened oval of her face framed in the hood.

The girl sat motionless in the grass, her expression frozen like a china doll.

"What is it, sweetheart?" asked her lover, still chuckling. Then suddenly he too noticed Sarah and his laughter choked off. The widened whites of his eyes glistened in the moonlight.

"Holy Mother of—" he muttered. He lifted the girl and dragged her backward until they were across the church yard. Then they turned and ran, clanging the gate behind them. As their voices faded into the night Sarah heard the girl sobbing, "A ghost. It was a ghost. I'll never again..."

Sarah's knees buckled. She dropped beside the bush, her head in her hands. Would her shaking never stop? Would her hammering heart ever quiet? Would she ever get home to bed where other decent women were at this hour?

At last filmy clouds veiled the moon, feathering the sharp contrast of fence and church. Sarah stole away and plodded the return path behind the houses.

Home at last, she entered the cabin and hung up her cloak. She crossed the room and pushed the wrapping paper into the cookstove. It ignited, sending dancing fire-shadows across her face.

"I've done it," she said. "I vowed to do whatever it takes and I've done it."

Sarah undressed and crawled into bed. Slowly her coverlet warmed and relaxed her tightened muscles. Her thoughts slowed. As sleep overtook her the image of the lovers, their staring, stricken eyes beholding a ghost, curved her lips into a languid smile.

While Sarah slept a dusky figure moved near the trees on a knoll overlooking the town. Pausing in dark blocks of shadow and flitting past light patches of moon-bright clearings, his hunched back created a curved outline against a slatted fence. He sneaked across a lawn and crept along the wall of a house. There, a string hung from an upper story window. He tied a piece of paper to the string, tugged on the string and waited.

Presently the string began a slow jerking journey upward and disappeared inside the window. Again he waited. The string descended. He untied its tiny bundle and melted into the blackness under the trees.

He could tell by the weight in his palm that he held a silver dollar. Enough to buy him plenty of 'white lightning' to warm his insides when the weather turned cold. He did not mind accepting the money, even though his work was tiring, staying up all hours of the night. If the judge wanted to pay him for watching the antics of that woman, well, that was fine with him.

There was just one problem jabbing him like a cheat grass sticker in his sock. He had seen so much of Sarah he was beginning to like her. She was a pretty woman and brave. Some of the things she said made good sense. He didn't like playing tricks on nice folks. Doing the judge's bidding was getting mighty uncomfortable at times.

Chapter Thirteen
THE DISTRIBUTION

Sarah jumped at the distant peal of the church bell. "Sunday," she mumbled. "Already it's Sunday morning. I have to go through with it."

She peered into the wavy kitchen mirror, pinned her hat to the soft bun atop her head and adjusted the feather.

"Come, Andy," she said, her voice sharp with anxiety.

They rode the quarter mile to the meeting house in silence. Sarah's fingers were tight on the reins. It had been her habit to prepare herself for services with quiet prayer. But not today. Today serenity was for someone else. Sarah's stomach lurched.

As they climbed the steps into the meeting house Sarah glanced furtively at the bushes. She hesitated.

"Come on, Ma." Andy touched her arm.

Faded blue curtains flapped listlessly at the windows. Flies circled the ceiling. In the family pew Andy squirmed with discomfort from the stiffness of his Sunday clothes. Sarah chewed her lip.

She watched Parson McKittrick as he stood behind the pulpit, alternately clearing his throat and rocking on his toes while the congregation filed in. The fringe of white fluff that encircled his bald head and blossomed on each side of his face looked like cotton stuffed behind his ears.

Sarah blinked and shifted her gaze to the floor. From the corner of her eye she saw the organist settle on the organ stool. The organ wheezed. "Guide Me O Thou Great Jehovah" the bellows intoned. Numbly, Sarah stood to sing with the congregation. But the melody stuck in her throat. Her tongue felt glued to her mouth. "...pilgrim through this barren land...Bid my anxious fears subside..." Yes, Lord, please. Would it never end? And then, too soon—too soon—it would be time...

Suddenly Sarah heard shuffling feet, rustling skirts and

discreet coughing. Andy, already seated, tugged at her skirts.

"Ma," he whispered. "Sit down."

The stubby organist waddled to her seat. McKittrick, riding his imaginary hobby horse, rocking on his toes, began his sermon.

"The spir-rit of the Lord is moving in this service," he boomed.

Sarah watched the sheen of perspiration spread over his scalp and down his cheeks. For a brief moment she wished it was proper for a lady to sweat. She saw the parson's ear lobes shake as his feet thumped the floor.

"Do you feel the Spir-rit, brother? Do you feel it, sister?"

Now his droopy eyes, resting on crescent-shaped pads of fat, peered at Sarah. She stiffened under his gaze and pinched her laced fingers together.

"I can fe-e-e-l it in my bones," McKittrick expounded. "I can fe-e-e-l it in my feet. I can—" He paused and pointed a finger at someone in the next row. "Sister, are your thoughts pure?"

The astonished woman stared at him, mouth agape.

McKittrick whirled away. The eyes of the congregation, weaving back and forth, followed his movements.

Sarah let out a silent sigh and looked at the mole beside his nose. It seemed to crawl when he spoke. The mole was a standing joke among the congregation. The children especially, liked to whisper with their mouths full of laughter, "There's a bug on the parson's face."

The mole shifted as McKittrick waltzed down the center aisle and punched a man's arm. "How about you, brother? Does your poor wife know where you were last Saturday night?"

The man's face turned red. His wife shot him a look of outrage then sat stonily erect beside him, staring straight ahead.

Sarah stirred on the hard bench. Her heavy skirts blanketed her legs. How she longed to lift them and let the air circulate. She glanced across the aisle. There, Judge Featherstone folded pious hands over the great mound of his stomach. His eyes were closed as if in prayer. But Sarah noticed his mouth pursed in a silent whistle. Little puffs of air escaped from his lips as he slept. Fright flared like tiny coals in her stomach. She forced her attention back to Parson McKittrick. Bubbles of spittle formed at the corners of his mouth. His voice rose in a mournful wail.

"My brothers, my sisters," he pleaded. His body began to shake. He snapped the Bible shut and fell to his knees on the rough plank floor.

Sarah saw Featherstone awaken, jerking his neck and looking cautiously around to see if anyone had noticed.

"There's a lake of fire awaiting," McKittrick moaned. "Oh, my brothers, do not delay."

A wave of uneasiness passed over the congregation. A few glanced speculatively at their seat mates. There was always a chance that McKittrick's ravings might hold a particle of truth.

It was time. Panic jabbed at Sarah's chest. Her heart began a double-time beat. She reached into her reticule, took out a handkerchief and pressed it to her lips.

"Come, Andy," she whispered.

Several people tossed sympathetic glances her way. She heard someone whisper, "Poor Mrs. Weatherby must not feel well."

As Sarah turned in the aisle she noticed Featherstone's foot protruding into the narrow space. She took a step. His leg moved. Their feet touched as her skirts brushed over the top of his boot.

She looked at him inquiringly and saw the venom swimming in his eyes. She could almost smell the aura of hostility that emanated from him.

Had he meant to trip her? She smothered a gasp behind the handkerchief.

The aisle seemed to have stretched since she sat in her pew. She looked toward the distant door. So far. It was like a gauntlet and she must walk it.

Behind her Parson McKittrick's voice became a hoarse squeal. "Oh, brothers and sisters, I beseech you..."

Sarah reached the door and seized the knob. Her heart hammered under her blue satin bodice. She glanced back. Featherstone was on his feet, his arms raised in petition. His broadcloth coat, straining at the seams, resembled a wrinkled tent thrown over a struggling bear. His ponderous voice sent vibrations down the rows of wooden benches.

"My friends," he began. "I have come to ask you to join me in calling God's vengeance upon certain heretics who stalk our land, leading their sisters astray. Notably that female thorn in the flesh, Abigail Duniway. Even in this fine community there are..."

Sarah and Andy passed through the vestibule and the door snapped shut. She breathed deeply of the hay-scented air as her skirts swept the steps of the meeting house. She set her jaw. Jake's warning stalked the borders of her thoughts. "What if it gets worse?" he had asked. "Is it worth it, Sarah?"

She shuddered, suddenly cold in the sunshine. She knelt beside the bushes. "Here, Andy. The papers are under here."

With icy fingers she pushed aside the sheltering branches and pulled out the sheaf of leaflets.

"Let's put one on each buggy seat and tuck one under the saddle blanket of every horse. We don't want to miss even one."

Andy held up a leaflet and began to read in a loud clear voice, "Husbands and fathers, women's suffrage must—"

"Hush, Andy, not now. You start on this side and I'll go to the far end. We'll meet in the middle. We need to be through before the congregation comes out. Hurry now."

Soon Andy stood beside her. "Mine's all done."

Sarah gave him a squeeze. "Good for you. I'm glad you helped me."

As she spoke the strains of "The Sweet By And By" wafted through the open windows. The men's bass notes thrummed like bull frogs. Sarah heard Mrs. Cariolla's valiant attempt to reach high E.

Andy said, "I betcha Pa would have helped us if he'd been here."

Sarah opened her mouth, then thought better of the remark forming on her tongue. "I don't know, Andy. Maybe. Now, let's get Lady started for home."

They climbed into the buggy. The meeting house doors burst open. The congregation spilled out like a swarm of contented bees buzzing among themselves. Sarah tickled Lady's back with the reins and they rolled through the gate and into the street.

She allowed herself one backward glance. Clusters of men and women stood reading the leaflets, astonishment written on their faces. The same breeze that carried the fragrance of freshly cut hay brought voices from the church yard. Sarah heard a guffaw. Two men struggled together. Parson McKittrick dodged their flailing arms and labored to pull them apart. The sunshine made his rim of white hair look like a slipped halo balancing over his ears.

And then Sarah's eyes met Featherstone's. He was leaning against his buggy, lighting his pipe and scowling at her. Thunder rolled in his expression.

Andy's remark echoed in her mind, "...if Pa had been here he'd have helped us." She suppressed the guilt that tweaked her conscience. No, Jake wouldn't have helped. He'd have given her a real dressing down.

She laid a hand on Andy's shoulder. "We don't need to tell Pa what we've done, Andy," she said, trying to make her voice casual. "He wouldn't be interested."

Andy turned serious eyes to her face. Innocence shone from his finely-molded features. "Wouldn't he, Ma? When he gets home I thought I'd tell him how I helped you. He'd be proud to know."

In the end she decided to tell Jake herself. The news had

crested flood-like on Front Street, washing other scandals aside. Better that Jake hear it from her than hear it garnished with gossip.

He was home, just in time for supper. Sarah stirred gravy in the heavy iron skillet as she talked. Jake clattered an armful of kindling into the wood box.

"You what!" he exploded.

"I said, I put women's suffrage leaflets on all the buggy seats while folks were still inside the meeting house."

Jake dusted off his hands with a resounding slap. His jaw worked. "Have you completely lost your senses? You deliberately used the meetin' house to further your own cause?" He shook his head. "How could you do that, Sarah? What made you do it?"

Sarah wrapped her apron around the skillet handle and poured gravy into a bowl. "I didn't exactly use the meeting house, Jake. It was the convenience of having all those buggies lined up together and..."

Jake paced the floor, his boots clomping on the bare boards. Sarah waited for him to pass before she set the gravy bowl on the table.

"But no one knows for sure that you're the one who did it?"

"Well, no, but—I guess they know nobody but me would—"

He interrupted. "Well, you're sure right about that. He rolled up his shirt sleeves. "I suppose Judge Featherstone was at the meetin' house?"

Sarah avoided Jake's eyes. "Yes," she murmured. Oh yes, he was there, wearing his sanctimonious Sunday face.

Jake scrubbed his cheeks with work-roughened hands. He took Sarah by the shoulders and shook her gently. She saw on his face anger and love engaged in a tug of war.

Abruptly he enveloped her in his arms. "My little wife, out to change the world. Fighting lions and tigers with her bare hands."

82

Sarah's ear was directly over his heart, her nose burrowed in his shirt. She inhaled his manliness, and the sweet pungency of his pipe tobacco. In that moment Phil seemed far away. Maybe things could be all right between her and Jake after all.

She whispered, "You're not mad at me then?"

He brushed his chin against the top of her head. "Mad at you? No, I'm not mad, I'm furious."

He held her at arm's length. "And I'm worried. Don't you ever stop to think what might happen because of these things you do?"

"Oh, really Jake, they don't—"

"Have there been any more threats since I've been gone? Did you find out who threw the rock through the window? You haven't planned anything else have you?"

She bit her lip. "Well, I—that is,—"

He misread her hesitation and sat heavily on a kitchen chair. "At least Andy won't have to know about this."

The door opened and Andy entered the kitchen. He limped toward Jake as fast as he could and hugged him around the neck. "Pa. Pa. You're home. Guess what Ma and I did at the meetin' house on Sunday."

Jake shot out of the chair. "Andy! You involved Andy in your scheme!" His eyes sparked with fury.

"Don't call it a scheme," Sarah countered. "That sounds so—"

"Well, that's what it is, isn't it? A scheme. You think you can change everybody and everything in this town. What's your next project? Advocating women mule skinners?"

"Jake, that's not fair. You know—"

"Well, I don't see why not. That ought to be just right for you. You can tramp up and down the street and holler 'Gee' and 'Haw' and—"

Sarah's face smarted. She saw Andy standing by the cabin wall, looking first at her then at Jake with frightened, bewildered eyes.

An awful lump formed in her throat. Hurt swelled in her chest. "Jake. Jake. Stop it!", she cried. "How can you talk to me like that? How can you be so hurtful?"

"I'm bein' hurtful? That's the small part of it. What I say is nothin' to what you may put yourself through. But you don't seem to care. You don't show any concern at all. Not for yourself or Andy or anybody else. Who knows what's goin' to happen next? Have you heard folks laugh at you on Front Street? Do you know they make jokes down at the saloon? Of course not. You don't care. You just go ahead. Keep makin' a fool of yourself and—"

Sarah heard the scream rise in her throat. She felt the cords of her neck tighten and her shoulder muscles contract.

"You, Jake Weatherby—how can you say these things? I never thought I'd hear such talk from my own husband. At least Phil cares for me. He wants to help me. More than you'd ever want to. I don't want to eat supper with you. I don't want to even look at you. You—you—"

She rushed across the kitchen floor, flung open the door and slammed it behind her. Tears blinded her as she stumbled onto the darkened path.

"Oh, God, why?" she sobbed. "Why doesn't Jake understand? Why does he say such cruel things to me? Is the whole town laughing like Jake says? Is that true? Oh, I don't know about anything any more. I just don't know."

Gradually her cries diminished. And as her emotions calmed, fragments of their argument echoed in her head.

She whispered to herself, "I told Jake that Phil cares about me. I actually said that to him. He made me so angry I just blurted it out. Now what'll he think? What will he—"

Standing there in the gloom, shivering, she watched Jake and Andy through the window. They sat at the table with the lamplight glowing on their faces. She saw Jake scrape the gravy bowl clean. Andy helped him clear the dishes from the table. Then Jake blew out the lamp.

A violent shudder shook Sarah's body. She paced the

yard, swinging her arms vigorously. Back and forth, back and forth, she tramped in the growing chill and darkness, until finally, she fell over a bush.

She got up and brushed herself off, gently fingering the twig scratches on her face. Exhausted and ashamed, she crept quietly into the cabin, undressed and lay on the edge of the feather tick as far away from Jake as she could get.

From out of the tense silence his voice sounded loud, "Kinda cold out there, isn't it?"

Chapter Fourteen
THE DON JUAN

When Sarah awakened the next morning, Jake had gone. "He left," she murmured. "He left without saying goodbye."

Somehow she got through the morning's chores, urging Andy to hurry as he fed Blossom's calf. "First day of school, Son. Don't be late."

"Wish I was a calf," he said.

"Why on earth would you wish a thing like that?" she asked.

"Wouldn't have to go to school."

"Oh, Andy, you're good at sums and you can read better than most boys your age. Why don't you like school?"

"Well, I kinda like it. But I like bein' outside with Pa better. Besides, he needs—needs somebody like me—somebody that understands him more than a—a woman does."

"Oh." So Jake had been filling Andy's head with that kind of talk. Sarah's face flamed with anger but she bit back the remark that burned on her tongue.

She sent Andy off to the schoolhouse with sandwiches and a boiled egg in his lard-bucket lunch pail. As she watched him limp down the path nostalgia swept over her for the days when she had been a teacher. She could almost feel the McGuffy reader in her hands and hear the boys arguing over whose turn it was to fill the water bucket. The girl's skirts would be rustling while they giggled shyly.

And she would never forget the scholar's eager faces turned toward her, shining with wonder and discovery. How satisfying teaching had been. How she had loved it. But she had given it up for marriage. Married women did not teach.

She sighed and filled the teakettle with water to wash dishes. As she stoked the firebox a knock sounded on the door. Sarah clattered the lid in place and smoothed her hair before she lifted the latch.

"Why, Phil. What a nice surprise." She felt the blush that spread upward from her neck, flushing her cheeks.

Phil stood there, grinning at her. "My friend, Sarah." And then, nonchalantly, "Jake gone again?"

"Y-yes. He is." She sensed her hands fluttering and clasped them tightly in front of her.

"How can that man just go off and—," Phil began, as if to scold. He paused, licked his lips and smiled. "Look at this, Sarah." He opened a paper sack.

"A Kodak. Oh, Phil. Where did you get it? Is it yours?"

"Yep, I sent for it. Remember at the picnic I told you I'd teach you how to use one?" He spread his arms wide. "Today's the day."

And Sarah, responding to the light in his eyes and the enthusiasm in his voice, repeated, "Today's the day."

She whirled around and turned the damper on the stove. "The dishes can wait," she said as she gave Phil a saucy smile.

They strolled behind the cabin into the pasture. Blackbirds pivoted and banked, swooping in an aerial ballet. The grass, grown dry and brittle, crunched pleasantly under their feet.

During the next hour Phil stood close, guiding her hands to operate the shutter. His hair occasionally brushed hers as he showed her how to squint into the lens. Their arms, warmed by the sun, touched from elbow to fingertip while he helped her steady the camera.

They chatted. They exclaimed. They laughed together. They snapped pictures until there was only one exposure left on the roll.

Sarah's cheeks glowed with pleasure. "I want to take a picture of that witness tree, Phil. It's such a majestic landmark, don't you think?"

He was slightly behind her, watching her with calculating eyes. "You're too close, Sarah. Back up about ten steps."

Obediently, Sarah walked backwards.

"There," Phil murmured in her ear. "That's just right." And his arms encircled her.

Sarah gasped. "Phil," she said weakly.

His moustache tickled her cheek. "Turn around, Sarah," he whispered.

She turned slowly in his arms. He took the camera and laid it on a stump.

"Sarah," he said, and kissed her.

The world reeled and righted itself. The roaring in her ears was replaced by a lumbering sound. Gradually Sarah realized the noise came from Big Lil's wagon rattling on the rutted road toward town.

Lil. She had forgotten this was Lil's day to take a crate of eggs to town and haul back pig feed.

Lil had seen it all. Lil, who always waved and hollered a greeting. Lil, who now sat chisel-faced, staring straight ahead.

Chapter Fifteen
THE DUTY OF FRIENDSHIP

Big Lil's rickety table jiggled as Sarah and Lil sat opposite one another, sipping raspberry shrub. Indian Summer heat waves shimmered outside the open cabin door. The cat lay stretched over the threshold, twitching his whiskers while he slept.

Sarah lifted the collar of her maroon calico shirtwaist to let air flow down her back. "But you don't know what it's like, Lil," she complained. "Jake's so preoccupied with his surveying, it's like his body comes home but his mind is still out there."

Lil said, "Humph."

"...and when he is home he's always finding fault. I can't do anything right. He says I favor Andy too much. He says if I don't quit working for women's suffrage something awful may happen. He says—and Phil understands. Phil makes me feel—"

She bit her lip, suddenly aware she had said too much. She took a quick swallow of her drink to hide her embarrassment.

Silence hovered in the air. Lil appeared lost in a muse. To cover the awkward pause Sarah changed the subject and assumed a chatty tone.

"Say, how's your ankle? My, that was a nasty accident you had. That nail must have been awfully sharp. Happened two or three days ago, didn't it? Does it bother you to walk? You really should go to see Dr. Barnaby right away. What if it gets infected? What if—"

She met Lil's gaze. What she perceived in Lil's eyes made her stop.

Lil's voice sent chills down her spine. "And you, Sarah? Do you take your own advice? You think Jake doesn't appreciate you so you play with that snake, Philip LeCour—"

"But, Lil—"

"Some day that snake will wind around your neck and strangle you. Then where will you be? You'll need a doctor more than I do then."

Lil's eyes glittered. She leaned across the table. "My sickness—I heal with herbs and prayer. Your sickness—", and she pressed a callused finger against Sarah's breast. "Your sickness is in here, in the heart."

Lil's eyes pierced Sarah's soul. Shame flooded her. Lil had penetrated the secret place where Sarah herself hadn't dared to look. She rose from the table and hurried to the door. She stepped over the cat and glanced back.

Big Lil sat stone-like, narrowly measuring her friend. Her eyes reminded Sarah of onyx arrow heads, pointing straight toward her.

Sarah walked stiffly from the cabin, leaving sharp imprints of her shoes in the dusty path. A muddy pool of half-thoughts and unfinished sentences eddied in her mind. Shame. Frustration. Anger and hurt. And above it all, the realization that she had deceived herself.

It was no use. No matter how she tried to rationalize, truth stood like a barricade in front of her. She couldn't get around it. Tears ran down her cheeks and she smeared them with the back of her hand as she reached her own front stoop.

During the next two days thoughts of Lil kept tapping at Sarah's mind. If Lil wanted to see her she could come here. She didn't have to go to Lil's cabin and listen to criticism. But another thought nagged her. What if Lil's ankle hadn't healed? What if she needed help?

Sarah sighed and pressed hard with her flat iron as she smoothed Jake's shirts. No, she would not go back to Lil's. She would not. And yet...

She finished the last shirt and set the flat iron on the back of the stove. Wiping the sweat from her face with her apron skirt, she sighed. "Oh, all right," she said. "I'll go, but if she says one word..."

She changed her dress, splashed cool water on her face and started out.

Lil's cabin looked deserted. Most days Sarah could see her in the yard, puttering in the garden or talking to her chickens.

As Sarah walked past the chicken house the hens flapped excitedly and crowded the fence. Their strident cackles screeched in her ears. A pang of anxiety stung her. Hadn't Lil been out to feed them? She ran the last few yards to the cabin and knocked.

"Lil. Lil? Let me in. It's Sarah, Lil. Can you hear me?"

The cabin was silent.

"Lil. Lil? Are you in there?"

She pressed her fists to the sun-warmed wood, letting her fingers slide down the door's leather hinges. What should she do? Was Lil in bed? A stick. That should work. A piece of wood to slip through the crack and lift the latch.

Sarah ran to Lil's wood pile, selected a piece of kindling and shaved a thin strip with the hatchet. She cut her finger. Hurry. Hurry. The strip split in two. Start over. Careful. Hurry. She ran back to the door and poked the splinter in the crack. It broke.

"Lil. Lil?" she cried. "Can't you come to the door? Please, Lil—"

Sarah pushed the blunted strip of wood into the crack again. She pressed her lips together in concentration. Just a little more and she'd have it. Now up. Push up. The latch lifted and the door swung open.

The air in the cabin smelled damp and stale. Lil sat at the table, a ragged quilt draped over her shoulders. An unnatural pink flared on her sallow cheeks. She stared dully at Sarah.

Sarah gasped. "Lil. Oh, Lil. I'm so sorry. I should have come." Remorse choked her throat. She bent to examine Lil's ankle and saw the puffy redness around the puncture wound.

"Have you soaked it, Lil? Did you apply a poultice?"

Lil stared into space, saying nothing.

Sarah looked around the kitchen. A pail of peelings ripened in a corner. Dirty dishes teetered in a precarious pile on the table. Beside the dishes sat a pan of grey dishwater, a grease rim congealing around the edges.

"Lil?" Sarah gently shook Lil's shoulder. The older woman struggled to speak through papery lips. "You came," she whispered. "My chickens. Need—"

"Yes, Lil. I saw. I'll take care of them. But first let's take care of you."

Sarah made her voice artificially bright. "We'll have you up in no time."

She kept up a steady banter as she laid wood in the cookstove, then ran to the pump for fresh water and filled a teakettle.

"I need a foot tub, Lil. Where's your foot tub?"

Lil mumbled something then closed her eyes and drew the quilt closer around her shoulders.

"I'll find it, don't you worry," Sarah sang gaily. She rummaged through the cabin, scouted around outside and finally spied the tub hanging from a peg on the cabin wall. Back in the kitchen she scoured a cup and found a tin of Amber tea.

"See, Lil? I'm using the teapot your ma gave you. The water will soon be ready. Ah, look at that nice steam. Now to rinse out the pot. And while we're waiting for it to steep we'll soak your foot."

Sarah set the tub in front of Lil's chair and poured hot water into it. "There now, we'll add just a little cold water so it won't burn your foot. Now then, in goes your foot. Put your foot in the tub, Lil. You can do it."

Still, Lil sat there.

Sarah lifted Lil's leg. "Mercy me. Is your foot made of iron?" She forced a false laugh. "My, but it's heavy."

At last she maneuvered Lil's foot into the water. Lil

bellowed and thrashed her foot around, sloshing water on the floor.

"Now, here's your tea. Just sip it slowly. That's the way. Good girl."

While Lil held the cup in both hands, Sarah eyed the bucket of rotting peelings. Her nose wrinkled. She leaned down to Lil's eye level. "I'm going out to feed the chickens while you drink your tea."

Lil's eyes traveled to the egg basket hanging on the wall.

Sarah nodded. "I'll gather the eggs too." She wagged a finger at Lil. "Now, don't you take your foot out of the water while I'm gone. Promise?"

Lil nodded.

Outside, Sarah threw the peelings over the fence and watched the hens scramble and fight for them. She filled the grain hoppers and the waterers, gathered the eggs and went back into the cabin.

The water in the tub had cooled. Sarah changed it. She brushed Lil's hair and rebraided it and made some cornmeal mush. Then she fashioned a poultice of thinly sliced potatoes. She applied it to the wound and wrapped it with strips of flour sacking.

Gradually Lil's eyes brightened. She began to limp around the cabin. "My hogs," she mumbled. "I couldn't feed them."

"Hogs", Sarah repeated, her face freezing in a hollow smile. "I'll take care of them before I go home."

She hugged Lil and made her sit down with her foot on a chair. "Won't take but a few minutes to feed those hogs. Anybody can do that. I'll go on home when I'm through."

She waved as she closed the cabin door and started down the path to the hog pen. "Anybody can feed hogs," she repeated to herself. "Anybody but me. Those smelly, fearsome beasts."

Beside the pen, she viewed the feed bucket with dread. She would have to empty it. The moistened grain was fermenting. She picked up the bucket, surprised at its weight. On the other side of the gate the hogs crowded close, squealing and jostling one another.

Sarah raised the latch and leaned hard to push open the gate. Some of the liquid sluiced from the bucket onto her skirt. The gate hook scraped across her arm. Then the gate slammed shut and the hogs surrounded her, pressing against her legs and shoving her toward the trough.

"Stop that. Ouch. Stop, I say. You dreadful beasts!"

Dirty snouts quested at her skirts, leaving muddy streaks. She swung the bucket. The mushy grain slooped into the trough. "There, eat it, you greedy things," she yelled above the din.

One hog had been squeezed to the rear. Now he dove between Sarah's legs and carried her forward. Her skirts fanned out over his ears like a bonnet.

"Oh, you brute! Let me down. Stop. Stop!"

She pounded his back and pulled at his bristly hair. Her legs were pinned by hogs pressing on either side.

"You awful things. Let me loose!"

At last she twisted and flung the empty bucket toward the gate. Then, inching backwards she worked herself off the hog's rump and fell into the dirt behind him. She snatched up the bucket, stumbled out of the pen and slammed the gate.

"Horrible. Horrible. Oh, my skirt. My shoes. Look at my shoes. Ohhh..."

Sarah fumbled with her shoe buttons. "I can't wear these clothes another minute." She kicked off her shoes, pulled at her stockings and peeled out of her dress.

Then standing uncertainly in white camisole and petti-coat, she rolled the discarded clothing into a ball. She would have to go home through the woods now. Nobody would see her there with the bushes and canary grass growing rank along the track.

The path wound between wild roses and around fallen trees. Birds chirped and flew ahead of her. Squirrels chattered.

If she hadn't felt so naked and dirty she would have enjoyed the stroll.

Presently Sarah entered a spot dimmed by overhanging branches. Beside the path a great willow drooped low, creating a cool, secret room that filtered sunshine and sounds.

In the sudden hush Sarah slowed her steps and walked softly. A furtive movement under the branches caught her eye. She glimpsed a flash of blue cloth, a girl's frightened face and a blur of pale skin.

She heard a whispered exclamation. In the next instant a man's flinty eyes stared into hers. She caught sight of long cheeks and a hard mouth.

Sarah cried out, "Mercy!" Her cheeks burned. She turned and ran.

She brushed past thorny bushes and leaped over logs. Out of breath, she finally reached the patch of canary grass that grew higher than her head. And blessed relief, there was the path worn smooth by deer and coyote and Andy's bare feet. In the distance, the chimney of her own cabin beckoned.

Soon she would have hot water to bathe. Soon she would put on a clean dress and comb her hair and be a human again.

Intermittently, the image of the man's insolent stare crowded her mind. A finger of apprehension slithered down her spine. Those eyes. She saw cruelty there. Something strange. Something evil. They reminded her of the hog's eyes—greedy, ruthless, ready to devour. She glanced over her shoulder. Were those eyes still watching?

Chapter Sixteen
THE DISPUTE

Sarah stood before the cluster of women in front of
McDougall's Mercantile. "But ladies, don't you see? When we
help one of our own it strengthens our cause. Each helping
hand becomes a rung on the ladder to women's suffrage."

A woman in brown calico spoke up, "They ain't one of
our own."

Sarah ignored her. "Surely we can find a little charity in
our hearts for someone in need."

The women peered from under their bonnets at her.
Their eyes were disapproving, their mouths downturned.
"Them Ruehl's are squatters. Them and their passel of
young'uns. Next time the sheriff makes the rounds he's gonna
kick 'em out."

Sarah made a pleading gesture. "But, what of the girl?
You tell me she's—"

"Ain't our concern. We didn't get her into the mess
she's in."

Sarah would not give up. "Surely we all could get a few
things together. Something to—"

"Give 'em something if you want. Won't be appreci-
ated. Folks like that don't know, don't care. Won't ever be
anything but what they are." The women turned from her,
clucking their tongues over her foolish suggestion.

Sarah was filled with frustration. Didn't these women
realize anything? If they were ever to gain the right to vote they
had to learn to help one another.

At supper that evening she decided to discuss the subject
with Jake. At least it would be a neutral topic they could talk
about. She found it hard to meet his eyes these days and wondered how much of her secret shame he read in her face.

"Why are the settlers so stingy, Jake?"

"Nothin' stingy about a settler," he said, stirring the gravy into his potatoes. "If your cabin burns down, they'll help you start another one tomorrow."

"Then why can't they show a little kindness toward the Ruehls?"

"Ruehls are squatters, that's why. They could get a piece of ground and earn their livin' by the sweat of their brow like everybody else if they wanted to. Folks don't have any use for cheaters. Settlers work hard for what they have. They figure others can do the same."

"But the children," Sarah argued.

"They figure the younguns'll grow up to be just like their elders. No use wastin' time on 'em."

Sarah couldn't let the subject rest. "The girl, Jake. She's just a child, they say, and she's in 'the family way'. Surely we could have a little compass—"

"I wouldn't worry about 'em, Sarah. Likely they'll move on to bless some other town. That's the way of folks like that."

Jake held a piece of bread between thumb and forefinger, sopping up gravy. "Where's Andy? How come he's not home for supper?"

"He's helping Lil. She hurt her ankle, but it's healing now. And Andy likes to help her. He—"

"Ought to be gettin' the wood in for mornin'. The boy had better tend to his own chores first."

The sharpness of his tone made Sarah clamp her mouth shut. And that was the end of the discussion.

The next day Andy came home from school with a torn shirt and scratches on his face.

"Ralphie did it, Ma. But it wasn't his fault. He said he was sorry. He even cried."

"Slow down, Andy. Who are you talking about? Ralphie who?"

"Ralphie Ruehl. He lives in a shack on the Bronstein place and old man Bronstein says,—"

"Mr. Bronstein," Sarah corrected.

"Mr. Bronstein—says he's gonna get the sheriff to kick 'em out 'cause they're squatters and—"

"But why are they there? What does Ralphie's pa do?"

"He steals chickens and apples and—"

Sarah's mouth fell open. "He what?"

Andy's tone was matter-of-fact. "Ralphie says his pa steals other people's chickens and apples and—" His eyes lit up with sudden remembrance. "Ralphie says his pa even stole a pig once. Dragged it home in a gunny sack."

Sarah applied tincture of iodine to Andy's scratches. It stung and she waited patiently while Andy howled. She brushed at the dirt on Andy's shirt. The tear was ragged. It would take some creative stitching to make the mend look neat.

"Now, sit down here, Andy. And let me get this straight. Everything you've told me—what does it have to do with your torn shirt and those scratches on your face?"

Andy shrugged. "It's nothin', Ma. Ralphie didn't mean to. Ralphie says sometimes his pa's home and sometimes he's in jail. And when he's home he's mean. He knocks Ralphie down. And he hits him—real hard."

"But that doesn't explain why he—"

"And today, when we were playin' in the school yard, Ralphie and me started wreslin' and—"

"You? Wrestling?"

"Yes, Ma. Other boys do it. I wanted to show I could too."

"But your leg. You—"

"I didn't hurt it. You can see I didn't. Anyway, Ralphie got me down." Andy's eyes sparkled with the telling. "You should have seen me, Ma. Ralphie said I did real good." Andy's finger traced a dirt stain on his overalls. "I guess Ralphie forgot it was me. He got to worryin' 'cause his pa's gettin' out of jail on Saturday and—and he said it was just like he was—was tryin' to keep from gettin' hit and—and he got too rough and..." Andy's voice faded away.

Sarah's indignation blossomed. "I should say he did. How old is this ruffian?"

"Ralphie's almost twelve. But he's not a ruffian, Ma. He's my friend."

Sarah's eyes narrowed. "Can't you find another boy to play with?"

"But I like Ralphie, Ma. It ain't his—"

"Isn't."

"It isn't his fault. He's different from the rest and—"

"The rest? How many are there?"

"He's got five brothers and they're always fightin'. Except for Salvia. That's his sister.

"And how old is she?"

"Ralphie says she's fourteen. And she stays home all the time."

"Why?"

"Ralphie says book learnin' comes hard for her. She never went to school. Besides, she's got a baby to take care of and—"

So this was the girl the settler's wives had talked about so scornfully. They hadn't mentioned she already had one baby. Sarah wanted to know more.

"A baby? At her age? Where's her husband?"

Andy shrugged. "I don't know. Ralphie says she doesn't have one. And he thinks she—she's gonna have a..." Andy looked at the floor. "And Ralphie says their pa sometimes beats and kicks her and..."

Andy stopped and rubbed his eyes. His shoulders slumped. He sighed. Sarah stared at him, her mind sorting the miseries of the Ruehls.

"Ma?"

"Yes, Son?"

"Sometimes I tell Ralphie he ought to run away. Him and Salvia. Just run away. Is it bad to talk that way? To tell him that?"

Sarah saw the troubled thoughts of a small boy who

wanted to help and didn't know how. She also saw her only son, who might have been hurt. She worked the cork back into the iodine bottle.

"I think, young man, you might remind Ralphie that you're only eight years old and you've had infantile—" She stopped.

Andy's eyes held a mixture of confusion and hurt. His lips quivered.

"What is it, Son? What's the matter?"

Andy's voice sounded strained. "You don't want me to be like other boys, do you? You want me to be different. You don't even want me to try. You're always after me to draw a picture of a man on a horse. I don't want to draw a picture of a man on a horse. I want to BE a man on a horse, Ma. Don't you see? I don't want to be different."

He limped to the door, gave her a sorrowful glance and ran out. Had she heard him right? Was this Andy—her son? Her crippled boy whom she had always sheltered?

She ran after him. He was hiking through the canary grass on the path that led to Lil's cabin. She opened her mouth to call him back, then let the sound die in her throat.

A fist closed around her heart. She sat down on a rock. Andy looked so small limping along the path. Presently the grass hid him from view.

How she used to worry that he would get lost on that path by himself. And Jake would snort at her, "Stop worryin', Sarah. The boy couldn't get lost if he tried. The grass is so tall you can't see out. There's only one path. One end leads to our place, the other one to Big Lil's. How could he get lost?"

And then she would go into her speech about him getting off the path. What then, Jake? He would snort some more and stomp across the floor in his boots. Then he would go out on the stoop, light his pipe and stare at the sunset.

Sarah turned and walked slowly back to the cabin. The Ruehls, that's who she should be thinking of. That poor young girl...Perhaps if she showed the other women by example...

Carefully, Sarah wrapped a loaf of bread in brown paper. From the bottom of a trunk she pulled out one of Andy's baby dresses. It was already yellowing.

She held it to her chest, thinking what a precious infant he had been. This would be a special present to Salvia, to let her know that her baby would be loved, regardless of circumstances.

Sarah fingered the lace and ran her hands lightly over the tucks. Hopefully, this gift would lead the way. The other women would soften their hearts and follow.

But Andy's words nagged at the edge of her thoughts. What kind of mother allowed her daughter to be beaten? What kind of father stole and treated his children so roughly? And why, oh why, was she the only one who wanted to go near them?

Chapter Seventeen
THE DUST-HEAP

Chickens scratched in the yard. A mongrel dog sunning beside the doorstep dug at the fleas behind his ear and eyed Sarah lazily.

She knocked on the cabin door.

A barefooted woman opened it a few inches and peeked out. "We ain't leavin'. You can't make us," she said.

"No. No," Sarah protested, risking pinched fingers as she held onto the door. "I've brought something for Salvia."

The woman's face poked through the crack, her ferret-like eyes searching as her long nose pointed at the package Sarah held.

"Well then, come in and light a spell."

There seemed to be children everywhere. Sarah glimpsed grimy faces behind tattered curtains, underneath chairs and around the table edge. Amid the clutter and confusion she looked for a place to sit.

On a corner bench a girl hugged a toddler sitting on her lap. Their eyes met. Something stirred in Sarah's mind, a flicker, a half-remembered impression. Then it drifted away like wisps of smoke.

Sarah was painfully aware of her own clean, rather stylish clothes. Perhaps she should have worn something older. She pushed some rags aside and sat down.

"Hello, Salvia. I'm Sarah Weatherby. I've brought you a present."

The mother's hands were already on the package, tugging it from Sarah's grasp. "What you brung?" she asked as she tore the paper.

Sarah wished she had not let go of the package. She wanted to give it to Salvia herself.

"It's a loaf of bread," Sarah said, "and something for the baby. I-I thought she might need it when..."

The mother held the baby dress aloft. Her eyes screwed up. "Humph. Pretty fancy for a bastard kid."

She pointed at the child in Salvia's lap. "She had that one last year. Now she's in 'the family way' agin. Ain't nothin' but a little slut. That man comes around her another time I'll blow his head off. I've whupped her and tole her git away from him but it don't do no good. She sneaks out when I ain't lookin'. Girl's nothin' but a bother anyhow. Boys now," and she spread her hands to indicate the row of dirty faces lined up before Sarah, "they kin work hard to pay fer their grub, then go out and raise brats of their own to help out."

Sarah watched as the boys stuffed wads of bread into their mouths. She forced herself to respond civilly. "Is there a piece left for Salvia?"

All of the boys grinned at her through the bread crumbs on their sticky faces and remained silent. And then, at the corner of her vision, somebody moved. Another boy! This one reached into the front of his overalls and pulled out a balled-up hunk of bread.

"She kin have this," he said, his eyes bright with intelligence. "I was savin' it for her."

It was Sarah's turn to stare. "Ralphie?"

"Yes, ma'am."

"You're Andy's friend, aren't you?"

"Yes, ma'am."

For a moment she shut out the other Ruehls and concentrated on Ralphie, who showed a thread of generosity. Ralphie — whose father beat him.

The boy handed the bread to Salvia, then knelt and tickled the baby under the chin. Sarah watched as the toddler held out his arms. She saw affection on Ralphie's face.

But the mother suddenly clapped her roughened fingers on Ralphie's shoulder. "Git on outside now. No use foolin' with that one." Her harsh voice rose, "Git on out, the lot of you. Air's too close in here."

The other boys scrambled for the door. But Ralphie

hesitated. He patted the baby on the cheek then looked directly into Sarah's eyes before he hurried away. Sarah returned his gaze, reading a silent plea for help in his expression.

As she strove for control of her emotions she gathered the torn paper from the floor and carefully folded it in her lap. Mrs. Ruehl's strident voice made her jump. "Can't sit here moonin' over Salvia. Got work to do." And without a 'thank you' or a 'good day' she strode through the door and slammed it behind her.

Sarah reached out and let the toddler take her hand. "May I hold him?"

Salvia nodded, her face hidden by her hair.

Sarah lifted the child. "My goodness, you're a big boy." She bent low, trying to make contact with Salvia's eyes. "What's his name, dear?"

"Isreel," the girl whispered. "Like in the Bible. Named him myself."

"And when will your next baby come, Salvia?"

The girl suddenly raised her head. Sorrowful eyes held Sarah's gaze. Her mouth twisted. Her body jerked. "Ain't gonna be no other baby. Ma says she'd rather see me die. Says she's gonna kill it."

A torrent of emotion poured out as the girl's fingers gripped, then pinched Sarah's arm. "Don't let her, Miz Weatherby. Don't let her. The babies, they's all I got. Don't let her kill it."

The words spent, Salvia hung her head again. Her tears fell into her lap.

"What of the man, Salvia? Does he love you? Where is he?"

Salvia's voice hardened and her hands clenched. "Naw. He don't love me. I ain't fooled that way. Not no more." She raised her head. "But he brings me things. And—and Ma takes 'em away. Won't let me have 'em.

"What things, Salvia?" Sarah stroked the baby's hair.

"Well, the first time he gave me fifty cents. Then he

brought me a pretty rock and a little bag of horehound candy and..."

Indignation flamed in Sarah's chest. She bowed her head over the little boy and rocked him. He put his hand up to her breast and relaxed against the crook of her arm.

With difficulty she kept her voice calm. "Tell me, Salvia, have you known Israel's father a long time?"

"Just since two summers past. I seen him in the store when I was with Ma. Next day I got a dozen settin' eggs from Big Lil. You know her? Ma ast me to. And when I came back he was waitin' for me on the path. Said he'd been watchin' how pretty I was. Said I was right pretty. Am I pretty, Miz Weatherby?"

Compassion welled up in Sarah. "Yes, of course you are."

Reassured, Salvia went on, "And he said if I'd meet him every time he wanted—and not tell Ma—he'd bring me a present." Salvia's mouth drooped. "But sometimes he forgets."

Unconsciously, Sarah reached for the girl's hand and stroked it. She prodded gently. "What is the man's name, Salvia? Is it anyone I know?" Heaven forbid that she should know the culprit.

Salvia's dark hair swayed sideways. "He don't live around here. He told me it don't matter what his name is. I could call him anything I wanted."

Sarah's mouth opened in shock. "You don't know his name?"

"No, ma'am. I just call him my man."

"But—your little boy—Israel. That man's the father of your son. Doesn't he want his son to know his name?"

Salvia shrugged. "He was kinda mad at first, said it was my fault. But he said, 'Yer ma'll take care of it. One more won't matter."

Anger bristled in Sarah's throat. "And now you're expecting another one and he—"

Salvia lowered her gaze to her lap again. "He don't

know about that one yet."

On a sudden impulse Sarah gathered the girl into her arms. "Oh, Salvia, Salvia."

At first she resisted Sarah's embrace. Then she relaxed against Sarah's shoulder. "I ain't had a body to care about me like this in a long time." Her plaintive voice was muffled in Sarah's dress.

"I know, child. I know." Sarah glanced at the baby dress Mrs. Ruehl had thrown carelessly across her chair. It seemed now such a useless, foolish thing to bring.

Sarah stood up and placed Israel in Salvia's lap. "Salvia, I want to help you. I don't know just what I'll do, but I'll think of something. Meanwhile," she bent down and made Salvia meet her gaze. "I want you to promise me you won't see this man again. Will you promise?"

"But I can't promise that, Miz Weatherby." Salvia began to wail as she rocked back and forth.

"Why not?"

"He tole me if I wouldn't meet him every time he wanted he'd—he'd beat me and—and—he said he'd tell it around that Isreel's pa was one of the boys in Nugget." She raised terror-stricken eyes to Sarah. "Please, Miz Weatherby. Please. I have to do what he says."

That night Sarah and Jake sat before the fire. Jake balanced his chair on its back legs with his stockinged feet resting on the nickel-plated stove fender.

"I'll have to use triangulation to meander that stream tomorrow. No tellin' how far it goes. Looks like pretty wild country up there. Wouldn't be surprised I'd have to hire another chainman. Calvin's skitterish in places where there's bear sign."

Sarah's needle wove in and out as she darned a sock. "Poor little thing," she murmured. "There must be some way - "

Jake's chair hit the floor. "You haven't listened to a word I've said. Might as well be talkin' to that owl out there hootin' in the tree."

Sarah was contrite. "I'm sorry, Jake. I can't get Salvia Ruehl out of my mind. I feel so—"

"What're you mopin' about her for? There'll be girls like that till kingdom come. Happens all the time. No use you—"

Sarah felt her temper rising. Her eyes snapped. "This one's different, Jake. Her mother doesn't seem to care a whit about her. And that man—he took advantage of her."

Jake shook his head. "Yeah, that's what they all say." He yawned. "Better get to bed. Day starts early tomorrow."

Sarah stared as the bedroom curtain swung shut behind him. Anger squeezed her throat. She might have known Jake wouldn't understand. What of other girls like Salvia? Folks just dispatched them to the dust-heap.

Sarah twisted around and gripped the back of her chair, her head resting on her arm. "Don't lose hope, Salvia," she whispered. "I'll think of something."

Chapter Eighteen
THE DOUBLE-DEALERS

Philip LeCour slipped into the woodshed behind the meeting house. The door creaked shut. It was dark. Phil hated the dark. Judge Featherstone's hoarse whisper made him jump.

"You're late. Anybody see you?" The judge struck a match between thumb and forefinger and lit a lantern.

Phil turned to look at him. "Couldn't help it, Judge. Nobody saw me. What do you think I am? Some kind of amateur?"

The judge scowled at LeCour. "Sometimes I wonder what you are."

The flickering light cast deep hollows under his eyes. "Why aren't you making progress with that woman? I want results. I demand results. If you think I'll pay you just to mark time, you're mistaken."

LeCour's eyes reflected the lantern flame. He gave the judge a lop-sided grin and stuffed trembling fingers in his trouser pockets. "You think I'm not getting anywhere? Is that it?"

"What I think is that you're getting sweet on her. She's softening you up instead of the other way around."

LeCour shifted his gaze. "No, Judge. That's one mistake I never make. I'd never fall into that kind of a trap."

"Well then, why haven't you persuaded her to do something? That's your 'forte', you told me. That's why I hired you. How can we smash this women's suffrage campaign if we can't hold her up to public ridicule?"

LeCour smoothed his moustache. "Well, I suggested that she sing a song in the saloon and—"

Featherstone snorted. "Sing in the saloon! She's no idiot, LeCour. I thought you knew how to handle women. If that's all you can come up with I'd better—"

LeCour jerked in alarm. The judge wouldn't dismiss

him, would he? Not now after he— "No, no, Judge. It just takes time, that's all. You'll see. Things'll go like you want. And we'll be sitting pretty."

Featherstone turned down the lantern wick. The deepened shadows reached toward LeCour from the dark recesses of the woodshed. He glanced about uneasily. "You gotta give me time, Judge. I can't—"

Featherstone's hand leaned heavily on LeCour's shoulder. His fingers dug into the flesh. "Show me results soon, LeCour, or I'll get somebody else to—"

"No. No. I'll deliver. You'll see."

The judge blew out the lantern. "You leave first. And remember, LeCour, if you try to double-cross me, I'll have you back in jail faster than you can blink."

LeCour pulled away and rubbed his shoulder. He opened the woodshed door, stepped out and waited for the creak and the click of the latch. Then he dodged from shadow to shadow. His body tensed as he peered nervously into dark alleys.

"Judge's getting pushy," he mumbled. "Wants me to hurry up, does he? Like to see him do anything himself. Women would all run away from him."

He reached his room and locked the door. 'You're getting sweet on her', the judge had said. Sweet on Sarah? The truth of the accusation made little knives turn in his stomach. LeCour groaned. Never before had he cared for a woman. He could turn his back anytime. Wouldn't bother him at all. But now...At first he was just play-acting like the judge wanted. And then it wasn't acting any more. It was real. He wanted her. Wanted her badly. And it made him hate Jake all the more.

LeCour grimaced at the very thought of Jake. That was why he had taken this job in the first place. He wanted revenge on Jake. It mattered nothing what happened to Sarah.

And now...His head ached. Those awful dreams...every night. Why couldn't he shake them? They were always the same. He closed his eyes and saw the scene behind his lids again and again:

Judge Featherstone was trying to push Sarah over a cliff. And he would be struggling, out of breath, trying to reach her in time, running, running...while Sarah screamed, "Help me, Phil. Oh, stop him. Please, Phil. Help me."

Then, just as he reached her with his fist knotted to strike the judge, he would awaken, sweating and panting. The judge's heinous expression and the terror in Sarah's eyes would linger in his mind for hours. Night after night the dream haunted him.

He needed revenge against Jake. But now he wanted more than that. He had to get Jake out of the way. Then maybe it could be just him and Sarah together. Alone. He hungered for her. One way or another he meant to have her, no matter who got hurt.

Let Featherstone go ahead and think he would help him bring disgrace on her. He could keep up the show. Then, when the time was right...

His palms were sweaty. Would Sarah have him? He had seen the look in her eyes...the way she tried to hide it. She wanted him too. All women did. It had always been so easy— and tiresome. But now it was different. He hugged himself in the darkness and in his mind he brought Sarah close.

Back in the woodshed Featherstone felt a tug on his sleeve.

"Well?" he said, jerking his arm away.

"The dandy's doin' fair, Boss. He's actin' like he's courtin' her and she trusts him. But I don't hear him persuadin' her to do anything outlandish."

Featherstone swore as he lit the lantern again. "That's what I thought. The double-crosser. Comes in here begging for more time and all along he's...So he thinks he can turn the tables on me, does he?"

"I dunno, Boss. But it does seem a shame somehow. Her bein' such a nice lady an—"

"You too? What's the matter with both you fools? If it wasn't for me you'd be begging on the street. You think somebody's going to hire a ragged hunchback? You're beholding to me and don't you forget it! Now listen up. I'm not waiting for LeCour. I have a plan and I want it done right."

He cleared his throat and turned the lantern flame down to a bare flicker. His whispers were muffled in the wind-driven tree branches that scratched the shed wall. A mouse scurried up the woodpile and stared at the two figures below.

The wind ceased momentarily as the hunchback cried out, "No. No, Boss. I can't do it. I can't. Don't make me."

Featherstone reached for the hunchback's collar. He raised him to his tiptoes and shook him. "You will, you hear? You will." He set the little man back on his feet and waited for the proper response.

"Yes—Boss."

"Good. Now go."

Featherstone snuffed out the lantern and waited. The hunched form paused in the doorway, silhouetted against a block of dusky sky. The door snapped shut.

Featherstone, blowing contempt through his nostrils, stood in the pitch blackness of the shed. Then he too lumbered out the door. The mouse twitched its nose at the lantern fumes and scuttled away.

Chapter Nineteen
THE DELUSION

Big Lil and Andy stood in the doorway of Lil's cabin as Sarah arranged her skirts on the buggy seat.

"Don't eat all of Lil's cookies now," Sarah admonished Andy, "And go to bed when she tells you."

"Yes, Ma."

Sarah watched as Lil put her arm around Andy and winked. She turned the buggy in a circle and called out, "I'll see you both at breakfast time in the morning."

The evening sun slanted low across the buggy. Golden glints reflected on Sarah's dress, deepening her emerald eyes and bronzing the tree tops.

She mentally reviewed the events of the past months with a feeling of satisfaction. In spite of all the threats and attempts at frightening her, the organization was growing. Tonight Ezra and Kate Henderson would join her group.

Just one thing marred her contentment. Jake did not share her dream. If only he wanted it as much as she did.

She turned into the Henderson's lane as the sun slipped behind the hills. Shades of violet and crimson spilled over the sky. A pair of Canadian geese circled, banked and landed on a nearby pond, rippling the purple water.

Sarah tied Lady to the hitching post and strode eagerly toward her friends in the open doorway. Their voices reached out to her, pulling her into the lamplit house. The door closed.

Across the road, hidden in the bushes, a small stooped man waited. He mopped his face and panted. Next time he would get a head start. Next time? He dreaded to think what his next assignment would be. He slipped through the shadows. Crouching low, he ran toward Sarah's buggy.

"Nice horsey. Nice horsey," he murmured. He sneezed. Lady twisted her neck and eyed him.

"Never you mind," he said to her. "I ain't gonna touch you."

He squatted beside the buggy and felt for the left front wheel nut. He hooked his wrench around it. It wouldn't budge. He gripped the wrench with whitened knuckles and bore down. At last the nut moved.

As he worried it loose he whispered to himself, "Gotta be just right so that it won't come off till she's away from here. How'm I supposed to know how much that is?"

He grimaced. Sweat made dirty rivulets down his face. "What if she comes out of that house before I'm through? What if this don't work right? Then where'll I be? Judge don't care. He don't care at all what happens to me. All he cares about is scarin' that woman so bad she won't get in his way any more. What kind of a judge is that?"

"The worst part comes after the wheel drops off. Then I have to catch her with the blanket. Drop it over her head. And tie her up and leave her in the woods. 'Just to scare her good,' the judge says. 'Won't hurt her none,' he says. And what if she don't want to get caught? Oh, the judge has an answer for that too. 'When buggy wheels come off,' he says, 'all women sit down in the road and cry. Or else they start walkin'. Either way', he says, 'it'll be easy'. Easy for him, of course. Sittin' up there in his parlor."

"And there's another thing. How long am I supposed to leave her out there? What if a cougar comes along?"

He remembered how the judge snickered at that question. "Getting squeamish?" he had asked, all the while twisting the hunchback's collar until he almost choked. Then he had bent down until his squinty pig-eyes were even with the hunchback's. "Leave her there until just before daylight. Then let her go. But don't let her see you. Untie the rope enough so she can work herself loose, then you scram."

Now here he sat with that horse watching him in the dark. Horses could see in the dark, couldn't they? Good thing they couldn't talk.

The hunchback sat on his haunches and wiped his brow.
"Wisht I could just start down the road and run away," he said to
the horse. Lady nickered softly. He stood up. "Huh, a lot you
care about it."

While he pocketed his wrench the door opened. Sarah
stood silhouetted against a block of lamp light. Her voice
carried through the still night air.

"I'm so excited about our plans. You've both been such
a help."

A man's voice said, "I'll see you to the buggy, Sarah."

The hunchback melted into the shadows beneath the
trees. He heard the man again, "You take care going home,
now."

Sarah answered, "I will, Ezra, and thank you."

The hunchback heard Sarah speak to the horse. The
buggy wheels crunched in the gravel. He felt for the blanket
and rope he left under a bush. Scooping them up, he ran along a
deer trail just inside the trees. "Have to be ready," he panted.
"Ready when the wheel falls off."

How he dreaded this job. He wished it wouldn't happen.
He feared he might be sick. Suddenly he raised his hand,
covered his face and muffled a sneeze.

The moon silvered the road. Sarah hummed a few bars
of "Blest Be The Tie". She was about to sing, "...our hearts in
Christian love," when an intermittent squeak intruded.

"What's that? What's making that awful noise?" She
pulled on the reins, slowing Lady and listening.

Bracing herself, she looked over the side of the buggy.
"Oh no, the wheel is wobbling!"

Tiny fear-points tingled the back of her neck. "Come
on, Lady. Get me home. Oh dear, will it hold?"

The buggy began to shake. The squeak became a
screeching complaint. Lady's ears twitched. She tossed her
head. Sarah's eyes shifted from horse to wheel and back again.

The road curved, then sloped downward through thick
trees and deep shadows. The buggy jolted over a rut. Sarah

watched in stunned disbelief as the wheel tilted then spiraled away. The buggy pitched violently. Sarah slammed against its side and tumbled into the dirt.

"Whoa, Lady! Whoa, girl!" Sarah screamed, her hands still holding the reins.

She scrabbled along the ground as Lady dragged the buggy forward. "Whoa, Lady! Whoa!"

The horse came to a jittery stop. Sarah crouched in the dirt. Her heart hammered. Her breath rasped in her chest. Slowly she let go of the reins and grabbed the side of the buggy, struggling to her feet.

"Oh!" she cried as pain knifed through her shoulder. Stepping on her skirts, she limped to Lady's side. "Good girl. Easy now. Easy. We're all right."

All right? Two miles from home, stranded in the dark and it was all right?

Her skinned elbows stung. She leaned against Lady, trembling, feeling the muscles under Lady's hide twitch.

As Sarah peered into the shadows she became aware of an eerie silence. Even the trees seemed to stand hushed, watching, waiting...

"We're going home, Lady," she whispered. "We're getting out of here."

She unhooked the traces with fingers that fumbled. The ache in her shoulder grew, spreading down her arm and across her breast.

At that moment a small figure crept silently across the road, his arms outstretched as he held an open blanket by its corners. Over his shoulder hung a coiled rope.

Sarah unhooked the breechin from the shafts. Her inexplicable fear grew. Prickles raced up her spine. She forced herself to walk Lady slowly forward until the shafts fell out of the hold-ups.

The small figure inched closer. The hunchback crouched, ready to spring. He raised the blanket and suppressed another sneeze.

Sarah head it; the merest suggestion of a sound, a pin-drop in the night. She whirled around and saw a dark block like huge wings descending.

Terror vaulted her onto Lady's back. She screamed. Lady lunged forward. Sarah's legs flailed the air. She yanked and tore at her skirts, trying to untangle the twisted fabric. At last she wrenched free and straddled Lady. The horse broke into a gallop. Sarah laced her fingers in Lady's mane. She leaned forward, her uncovered legs squeezing Lady's flanks.

"Home, girl. Take me home," she cried.

The road, the trees, the shadows all shot past in a moon-lit blur.

"I mustn't fall off, mustn't fall off," Sarah whispered hoarsely. Her fingers felt like sticks. Her leg muscles cramped. She cringed low over Lady's back, waiting in panic for the monstrous claws that would surely snatch her into the air.

Far behind, the little man stood in the dusty road. He threw the blanket on the ground and kicked it. The judge would have his hide for sure. The judge never tolerated failure. But how could he have guessed Sarah would jump on the horse bareback? And straddle it like a man?

She was a plucky one. He was not sure who he scared more—Sarah or himself.

He lowered the scratchy rope from his shoulder and flung it away. "No more," he said. "I won't do it any more. I'm through. I'm not goin' to bother that woman again. If the judge wants it done he can do it himself. I wisht I hadn't ever started. Somebody ought to stop that judge. It ain't right. Ain't right at all."

Hands in pockets, he hiked the two miles back to town. He crept quietly to the house on the hill, tied his message on the string and slinked into the shadows. There would be no money for him tonight. And he sure was not going to hang around and wait for old pie-face to explode.

The imported grandfather clock in Judge Featherstone's

sitting room chimed nine times. He wiggled his toes inside his carpet slippers and stretched.

"Ahh. Nine o'clock." He lifted a cup of coffee to his wrinkled lips. "That hunchback ought to have his business wrapped up by now." He chuckled to himself at his clever pun. His stomach jiggled with laughter. "I never used that old blanket anyway. Wonder how hard she fought him? She looks like the feisty type for sure."

He yawned and swallowed great draughts of coffee. "Not that it matters. I'm safe enough. Nobody would ever connect such activity with me. And even if the hunchback gets caught—well—who'd believe anything he says?"

Featherstone rose ponderously. Puffing with exertion, he crossed the room. "It certainly has taken time getting that woman out of the way. But I have things pretty well sewed up now. I'll pay someone to get rid of the hunchback and then I'll see to it LeCour goes to jail where he belongs. With that woman's silly campaign sidetracked I'll make my move for the state house."

He took a few coins from his pocket and slipped them into an envelope. The floorboards protested under his weight as he opened a door into a darkened room at the back of the house. He padded across to the window and raised the sash. The coins made a muffled clink as he laid the envelope on the sill.

The evening's cool breeze wafted into the room. The judge lowered himself onto a Chesterfield, easing his flabby bulk into a relaxed position. As he waited for the familiar tug on the string he began to hum, "I was seeing Nellie home, I was seeing Nellie home..."

It seemed to Sarah that she had clung to Lady's neck for hours. The wind screeched past her ears. Lady's frightened gait jarred and bruised her bones and flesh. And then, just as she knew the ride would never end, Lady stopped.

Sarah opened her eyes and lifted her head. She saw the corral gate. Lady had brought her home.

"Thank you, Lady. Thank you," she rasped. She tried to get down. Her legs were rubbed raw. Her joints felt locked in place, welded to the contours of the horse. Moving slowly, she eased herself down Lady's heaving side. Her dress, wadded and dirty, bunched up around her waist.

"Open the corral gate," she told her sodden brain. Woodenly, she staggered to the gate and opened it. She grasped Lady's bridle. "Walk the horse," she said in a monotone.

Around and around the corral they went. Here there was no fright, no winged apparition. There was peace and the gentle clop, clop of Lady's hooves. When Lady ceased to blow and the sweat scum dried on her coat Sarah led her into a stall. She poured oats into the manger and listened to the rustle of Lady's velvet nose nuzzling the grain.

Sarah's hand lifted the curry brush from the wall and with wide sweeping strokes she groomed Lady's coat until the hair was soft and gleaming in the lantern light. Peace. Comfort. Safety. Methodically, Sarah combed Lady's mane and tail. She blew out the lantern and shut the barn door.

With staring eyes, she glided out of the barn, through the corral, up the path to the cabin and let herself in.

She lit the kerosene lamp on the kitchen table. Still gliding, she went to the mirror above the bench where the wash pan sat.

Who was this woman in the mirror? Dirt-caked face, hair askew, rag of a dress. How dare she stand in this kitchen? She grasped her dress by the hem and raised it high over her head.

A jagged pain knifed her shoulder. She suppressed a moan. A stifled scream tore at her throat and started a throbbing ache in her chest. She ran to the bedroom. Under the cocoon of the quilt she grew quiet, hearing only her heart's steady thump and the brush of her eyelashes against the pillow.

The lamp on the kitchen table kept silent vigil. The oil burned low. The flame went out.

Chapter Twenty
THE DECEPTION

Blossom's insistent lowing sounded through the broken window, rousing Sarah from her escape of sleep. Surprised, she opened her eyes to the morning brightness. She eased out of bed. In the kitchen she frowned at her soiled dress that lay in a heap on the floor. She opened the cabin door, dipped rainwater from a barrel under the eaves and dropped the dress in a tub.

Moving carefully, she took the milk pail from its bench and limped to the barn. As she milked Blossom, each squeeze of her hands brought pain. It tore, ragged-edged, along her shoulder muscles.

She leaned her head against Blossom and tried to sort the nightmare of jumbled images that flooded her mind. She had not imagined last night's terrible fright. It had gripped her with steel bands, wringing her senses. It was real.

She made herself remember, sifting the details, pondering... After she left Ezra and Kate...When did she first hear the squeak?

The buggy tipped. She fell out. A sound. There was a sound. It was like a...She closed her eyes, probing, thinking.

Blossom flicked her tail across Sarah's face and tickled her nose.

"A sneeze!" she said triumphantly. "It was like—like somebody trying to suppress a sneeze. I whirled around—those huge black wings came at me and..."

Blossom chewed contentedly. Flies swirled in a shaft of sunlight. Sarah eased the full milk bucket from under Blossom and turned her out to the pasture. She inhaled the mingling smells of hay and weathered boards as she stood in the barn doorway.

Over the dappled field a breeze rippled the grass like waves on a body of water. Sarah watched it idly, frowning in concentration. An impression flitted through her mind: *It looks like water but it's grass. Things are not always what they seem to be...*

Suddenly she cried out in alarm. The lost buggy wheel was no accident. Someone deliberately loosened it. The giant wings were...canvas? Or cloth. And the other movement? Why, it was the legs of someone who held the cloth, ready to drop it over her.

It was likely the same person who had done all the other things—the rock through the window, the corn husk doll, the...She had an enemy stalking her, someone who went about his dirty deeds methodically. Someone who hated her.

Jake must not find out. He would forbid her to work another day for women's suffrage. Somehow she must keep the whole frightening incident a secret.

The blacksmith would repair the buggy. She could pay for it with the money she saved from teaching school. Thank goodness, Jake had insisted she keep her earnings.

She shuddered, leaning against the barn door. She closed her eyes. Could she go on? By herself? Knowing?

"I will not be afraid, " she said with a tremor in her voice. "No matter who is trying to hurt me. I won't be afraid."

Lil's call broke her reverie. "Halloo, Sarah. Is breakfast ready?"

Sarah hurried. She shut the shed door so Lil wouldn't notice the buggy was gone. Trying not to limp, she carried the milk to the spring house. In the cabin she mixed pancakes for Andy and Lil. They chattered between bites, laughing and teasing one another.

Occasionally Sarah caught Lil's curious glances but pretended not to notice. She thought she played the charade well until Lil said, "Better mix up some honey and vinegar for that rheumatism, Sarah."

After Andy went home with Lil to help shuck corn Sarah walked into Nugget. At the door of the blacksmith's shed she paused.

The blacksmith called to her, "Be right with you, Mrs.

Weatherby."

Sarah watched him thrust a piece of iron into a fiery nest of coals. He worked the bellows of the forge and the coals winked and glowed. Sweat glistened on his muscular arms. Fascinated, Sarah saw the iron yield under his hammer blows, bending and shaping to his plan.

He plunged it into a bucket of water. As it sizzled and faded from orange to purple Sarah told him her story.

Her tale was simple. The wheel had come off her buggy while driving home from a visit with friends.

The blacksmith said, "Surprised Jake hadn't checked the wheel nuts."

Sarah looked at the floor. "I guess—guess he forgot." She hated the lie. It sat on her tongue like an unpleasant taste. "You don't have to repair the buggy here, do you?"

The blacksmith wiped his hands on a greasy rag and looked at her blankly. "You want me to fix it at your place?"

Sarah shifted her feet. "Couldn't you just put the buggy in my shed and bring back the part that needs repair and..."

"Maybe I can and maybe I can't. Depends, Mrs. Weatherby. Probably just a broken whiffle tree. That's easy enough to fix."

Sarah studied a trickle of sweat wending a grimy trail down his arm. How could she make him understand? Finally, she blurted, "I don't want Jake to know."

The blacksmith's eyebrows shot up.

"And I want you to make it look just the same. So—so that no one can tell the—difference. And—and when you're finished would you bring it to my place after dark? I don't want anyone to see..."

She plowed on before she lost her nerve, "One more thing. I have the money. I can pay you. We won't need to bother Jake."

She pleaded with her eyes, willing him to understand. The blacksmith looked more puzzled than ever, but he agreed.

"Yes," he answered each request. "It's a simple matter.

One a wife can take care of herself. No need to bother Jake. Yes, Mrs. Weatherby. If that's what you want, Mrs. Weatherby. You have my word."

She thanked him and turned away. Her steps matched the rhythmic pounding of his mallet. She looked back and saw him standing in a shadow, scratching his head and watching her.

Out of town, she allowed herself to limp. Unbidden, the ghost of her conversation with Sam Withers, the printer, came to haunt her. Sam had pleaded, "No need is there, Mrs. Weatherby, to tell who printed these?" She had replied, "No, Sam, no need."

Now her request to the blacksmith echoed: "No need to bother Jake with it." And the blacksmith's answer, "No, Mrs. Weatherby, no need."

Last night she was so confident. The work was going well. But now, her efforts teetered as precariously as a tall stack of building blocks. One word of betrayal from the blacksmith could bring them tumbling down.

Chapter Twenty One
THE DEAFENED EAR

Another week passed. Jake had not returned. While walking home from Lil's one day Sarah saw Phil LeCour waiting for her on the doorstep.

"Phil. You shouldn't be here. What if—"

"Someone should see me?" He finished her sentence.

Lately Phil had begun to irritate her. He was changing. He wasn't the man she first met.

Phil persisted. "Who cares if we're seen together? Don't you think it's about time we—"

Sarah brushed past him and flung open the door. Her skirts swirled about her as she stepped into the cabin.

Phil followed and enclosed her in his arms. He nibbled her ear and whispered, "I was just thinking how nice it would be if this was my cabin and you were coming home to me."

"Stop it." Sarah squirmed free and put the table between them. "Phil, you mustn't talk like that."

He followed her around the table. "Why don't you quit pretending, Sarah?" The edge in his voice surprised her. "You know you care for me."

"Don't say things like that. I never intended us to...I think you'd better leave."

Phil's eyes had a flinty look. "How many days is Jake overdue?"

"A week. It isn't your concern anyway, Phil. Please go."

"Maybe he isn't coming home."

Sarah went to the window, opened it and let the casement rest on its wooden pegs. "He'll be here," she said with conviction.

Phil studied his fingernails. "Maybe. Maybe not." He stood beside her. "Suppose he likes being away. You ever think of that?" He caressed the back of her hand where it rested on the windowsill.

Sarah swiftly slipped her hand from under his. "Whatever do you mean?"

Phil's face was close to hers. "I meant only that maybe Jake decided not to come back. Maybe he thinks he's better off staying away. After all, a surveyor's life isn't much account for a married man and—"

"Phil! How could you say such a thing?"

He shrugged and turned to look out the window. "If I had this place, first thing I'd do is cut down that old tree."

"The witness tree? You couldn't. It's still part of the legal markings for our property."

Phil's eyes held steely depths. "Legal, bah. Wouldn't bother me. I'd cut it down. That old tree irritates me every time I see it."

His finger explored the shoulder seam of her dress. Sarah held her breath and suppressed the quiver his touch incited.

"If I had this land I'd sure do a lot more with it than old Jake."

"Jake's not old. I asked you to leave, Phil. Now go."

"He's older than me. I'm closer to your age, Sarah." He looked at her throat where her pulse trembled. He pried her fingers from the window ledge and draped her hands over his shoulders.

She tried to push away. "Let me go. Don't—"

Phil held her tightly. "Come on, Sarah. Give me a hug."

Sarah twisted her head. "No, Phil. I don't want you to kiss me."

"You don't want my kiss?"

"Don't talk about kissing. Go away. Just go away..." Her conflicting emotions were smothering her.

"Ah, Sarah. Don't be cross. I was just rambling, that's all. You know how it is to ramble?" His lips touched her throat.

"No, Phil. Stop it. Stop, I say!"

LeCour imprisoned her in his arms. "A little ramble here, a little ramble there, a little—"

Suddenly a clatter of hooves sounded in the lane. Phil released her. His face changed instantly. Sarah caught the hooded menace in his eyes as she turned to peer through the window.

"It's Crandall," she said on a shaky breath. "One of the chainmen. He must have news."

Phil backed away quickly. He climbed to the loft and lay still. Sarah smoothed her hair and arranged a calm expression on her face. She opened the cabin door.

"Hello, John."

John Crandall's face was sweat-streaked. His clothes were caked with dust. "Afternoon, Mrs. Weatherby. No need to be alarmed. Jake asked me to ride on ahead. He thought you might be worried. Said he'd be along about four o'clock tomorrow. We ran into a little trouble. Nothin' to get upset about. He'll likely tell you about it when he gets home."

Sarah swallowed. "You've ridden hard, John. Won't—won't you come in for a cool drink before you go on?" She had to offer. But what if he saw Phil? Did he notice anything different about her? She felt guilty, so guilty...

She hardly heard John's answer. "No thank you, ma'am. I want to get on home. I expect the family will be waitin' to see me. Jake's a fine man, Mrs. Weatherby. I know you must miss him when he's gone like this."

Would he never go?

Sarah nodded. "Y-yes," she said. Her neck was stiff. She tried to smile but her face felt carved with shame. She stood at the door and watched until horse and rider were a mere blur of movement and trail dust. Behind her she sensed Phil's presence. She felt his lips on her neck.

"Don't do that! Get out!" She whirled to face him.

He shrugged and began to pace the floor. A restless excitement came into his eyes.

"Four o'clock tomorrow," he said. "That right, Sarah?"

"Yes, you heard what John said. And I want you to—Why are you looking like that? What are you thinking?"

"You'll see. Just you wait and see." His eyes grew wild. "You'll see." He danced outside and down the path.

Sarah stared at him from the doorway. "What's got into you, Phil? What are you talking about?"

"You'll see, Sarah my love, you'll see." He strode away.

Sarah covered her face with her hands. She felt lightheaded, as if she were spinning out of control, sinking into a whirlpool.

"What's he up to? Nothing he said made sense." She touched the back of her neck where his lips had brushed her skin. She shuddered. "He won't leave me alone. I don't think he heard a word I said. It's as if he's determined to be deaf."

Evening came at last. Sarah prepared for bed. She bolted the door and blew out the lamp. Gradually she relaxed on the feathertick. Her hands were stained from peeling apples and slicing them to dry for winter fruit. Her back ached.

Tomorrow Jake would be home again. She was grateful there had been plenty of time to get the buggy repaired and to let her bruises heal.

Sleep overtook her tired body.

In the night a tapping at the door awakened her. Cautiously she padded across the floor. If it was Phil she positively would not let him in.

"Who is it?" she asked in a low voice.

"It's me, Jake. You suppose my wife'd let me into my own cabin?"

Sarah slipped the bolt and flung the door wide. "Well, of course. How could I know? John said you wouldn't be home until tomorrow."

"Didn't take as long as I thought. And I made Moses hurry. That old horse can lope along pretty good when he's headed for home. Got any grub I can eat? I could down a jack rabbit."

The following afternoon Philip LeCour climbed the bluff and watched the gap for two hours. When he finally gave up and sneaked back to town he spied Jake at the cobbler shop, trying on a pair of boots. As LeCour loitered, hidden by a wagon load of lumber, he heard Jake's deep voice: "Yep. Got back about midnight last night. Sure felt good to crawl into my own bed after sleepin' under the stars for two weeks."

LeCour cursed under his breath and ground an ant into the dirt with his heel.

Back in his hotel room he threw his rifle on the bed and gritted his teeth. He stood behind the flimsy curtain and watched Jake cross the street. His hands clenched and unclenched as he said, "Right between the shoulder blades. That's as good a place as any. And then it'll be just Sarah and me..."

Chapter Twenty Two
THE DISCLOSURE

Jake and his old friend Eb Scribner sat near the cabin doorway to catch the breeze. Sarah set a pitcher of raspberry shrub on the floor between them. They filled their cups and talked.

Behind them Sarah sorted dry beans at the kitchen table. The beans made a rhythmic rattle as they fell into a bowl.

"How many years you been surveyin, Eb?"

Eb looked toward Nugget. "Let's see, started back in '68. That makes about twenty years, don't it? I just worked my way west as the territory opened up."

Jake took a swallow of his drink. "You measure to the center of a bearin' tree, don't you?"

"Well, I'm mighty good at guessin' sometimes. Most times I measure to the face of the blaze."

Jake disagreed. "Seems to me the best way is the middle of the tree. After all, to my way of thinkin', from the corner to the center of the tree is—"

Eb interrupted, "Depends. Depends. The slope distance's got somethin' to do with it, you know."

Jake refilled Eb's cup. "How many chainmen you got?"

"Three. Two's good men. The third one ain't. Sure glad to be gettin' back in the field. Last year's depression was tough. Larder got so bare even the mice moved out."

"You use a two pole chain?"

"Yeah. Used a five at times. But Rufus, he's my forward chainman, he gets mixed up with the five and we have to go back and do it over. Curses, I could wring his neck when he does that. Sometimes he's so drunk he can't see where the tally pins are. Once he stumbled over one or we would've lost it."

Jake's eyebrows raised in surprise. "Why don't you let him go and hire somebody else?"

"Can't. He's the Missus' brother."

Jake thought he had better steer a slightly different course. "You ever use the new steel tape? They say it's a real time-saver."

"Yeah. But I don't hold much with new-fangled things. Betcha that tape gets caught in the bushes. I don't care to save time anyway. When I get home the Missus fusses at me. Just as soon be out under the trees somewhere listenin' to the song-dogs argue. Money don't matter. Keeps me in beans and bacon, that's about all."

He drained his cup and went on talking. "Worst chain-man I ever had was that LeCour fellow. Never saw a more worthless human bein' on the face of the earth. How he became a deputy surveyor, I'll never know. Musta paid somebody off to get that job." Eb shook his head and looked at the floor.

Jake heard Sarah gasp. He glanced back. Her hands were suspended in midair over the bowl. An expression of intense pain like the jagged edge of lightning flickered across her face. Jake opened his mouth to inquire of Sarah but Eb's voice pulled him back to their conversation.

"...land office told me LeCour falsified more claims than any other surveyor they ever saw. Took bribes, he did. Shame-less, that's what."

Eb worked a match out of his pocket and turned it over in his hand. "Did some dirty work against you too, didn't he, Jake?"

Jake paused before he answered. He stole another glance at Sarah. She stared at the bowl of beans with whitened face.

Jake dragged his attention back to Eb. "Oh—LeCour? Seems a long time ago now. One of my chainmen caught him in time. Had his axe raised. Tried to cut down the witness tree at the corner of my property.

"Seems he was schemin' to make my claim look false and when it came time for me to prove up, they'd throw it out. Then he planned to buy it up. Didn't work though. Think he's been sore at me ever since. Probably blames me for the years he spent in prison."

Eb took a pouch out of his pocket and cut off a hunk of tobacco. "Yep. Fellow like that's nothin' but mischief. Hope they keep him there."

"He's out, Eb."

"Out? How'd ye know?"

"Saw him at the picnic in Dimlar's Grove."

"You can bet he pulled some strings then. The ornery bugger's probably chasin' some female, else he wouldn't be hangin' around. Always did favor the ladies, that one."

Eb got up and stood in the doorway. He aimed tobacco juice at the gooseberry bush beside the cabin wall. "Won't have to worry about the bugs botherin' that bush of yours, Mrs. Weatherby." He sat down again.

Jake felt the silence behind him. Uncomfortable, he shifted in his chair. He stood up and stretched his long, lean body. Nothing seemed to help. Even his neck had a crick in it. And his muscles were all bunched up like he was ready for a fight.

He wished Eb would leave. He enjoyed the old man's ramblings. But now, somehow the conversation annoyed him. He couldn't put his finger on it. But the irritation was there, like a tickling hair he couldn't brush off his face.

Eb leaned back in his chair. "Say, Jake, ya hear how they're measurin' back in Kansas? Heh, heh. Quite a trick, that. All they do is load a passel of rocks on a wagon and tie a white rag to the back wheel. Fella trots alongside watchin' the rag. Ever time it goes around he gives the signal and a fella ridin' in the wagon throws a rock out. Ain't that somethin'?"

Jake frowned. "Don't know if I'm ready to believe that one, Eb."

Eb shrugged, "I dunno. It's makin' the rounds anyhow." Wouldn't work in this country. Too many trees and boulders. Well, I best be gettin' on home. Got a section I'm workin' on over Rose Hill way. Startin' off at sun-up tomorrow."

He turned to Sarah. "Thanks for the drink Mrs.

Weatherby. Hope all this talk ain't offended you none."

Eb shook hands with Jake and stepped outside. Jake stood on the doorstep and watched him ride out of sight.

He heard Sarah rise from the table. Her hand felt like ice when she touched his arm. "Why didn't you tell me about Philip LeCour before?" Her voice was a moan of distress.

"Guess I never thought to. All that was over and done with before you and Andy came West. And then LeCour was gone and..." He put his arms around her. "...and I didn't suppose you'd be interested."

There was something in her eyes. He couldn't read it. A sadness? He remembered the flicker of pain he had seen earlier. She still looked pale. "Sarah? What's wrong?"

She closed her eyes. "Hold me, Jake. Hold me tight. Please."

"Always glad to oblige a lady," he tried to joke. But she didn't smile and as he folded her trembling body close apprehension stabbed him.

Snatches of talk he had heard in Nugget flooded his mind. Street-corner gossip bored him and he usually made a point of ignoring it. Suddenly it dawned on him how the talk always started after he passed by or turned his back. He pressed his cheek to Sarah's and squinted his eyes, struggling to resist the memory of it. Still, the words pierced his thoughts:

"Did ya see 'em in the buggy together?"

"Close as two peas in a pod."

"He goes out there regular as clock work when the Mr. ain't around."

"That dandy knows a easy mark when he sees one."

It couldn't be. Couldn't. It was unthinkable. And yet...A lump as big as a pine knot stuck in Jake's throat.

Sarah heard his ragged intake of breath. She felt his muscles stiffen and the rumbling vibration in his chest as he spoke, "I'm leavin' in the mornin'."

She nodded. Had she opened her mouth a cry would have escaped. She would not allow it. Mortification clung to

her like shackles. A smothering guilt covered her. She fanta-
sized a newspaper headline: "Surveyor's wife enticed by local
felon!"

"I-I need some air," she managed to mumble and swayed
toward the door. She wandered in aimless circles around the
cabin.

The routine of habit helped her prepare supper and put
Andy to bed. She could only pretend to sleep. In the morning
Jake rode away. She did not meet the question in his eyes, nor
did he ask it.

After Andy left for school, Sarah attacked household
chores. With savage strokes she scrubbed floorboards and beat
rugs. She kneaded bread dough with uncommon fervor.

"I'll work 'til I die," she muttered through dry lips. "I
don't care what happens to me. What difference does it make?"

Chapter Twenty Three
THE SITTING DUCK

The days passed slowly. Sarah drowned her emotions in numbing toil. Friday came. Jake would be home in the evening. As Sarah cleaned the glass chimneys of the kerosene lamps LeCour sauntered through the door.

Sarah gasped. Her heart raced. She had rehearsed a thousand times what she would say to him. Now no words came.

LeCour pulled an envelope from his pocket. "Here it is," he said triumphantly. "Our snapshot."

The snapshot! It was like a slap. She had almost forgotten it. She glanced at it. There they stood, grinning like old friends.

"Why did you keep this? Phil, you've deceived—"

He did not listen. "Don't we make a handsome couple? We belong together, Sarah. Anybody can see that. We need each other."

"No, Phil. You mustn't—I want you to go—"

"We'll show it to Jake. He'll understand. A woman gets lonely when a man's always off surveying some old—"

"No, Phil. Don't you dare show that to Jake. You know that picture means nothing!"

He paid no attention to her protests. His hands were shaking her shoulders. "Jake'll be home this afternoon, won't he?"

"Yes. And I want you to be gone. I want you to leave."

"Coming through the gap, isn't he?" LeCour's voice hardened.

"Of course. Where else? But you must get out—"

"The gap," he said. "The gap," he repeated. He laughed.

"Phil," she cried. "Listen to me. You and I—"

"Don't worry, Sarah," he interrupted. "We won't have to

show him the snapshot. Never thought it would be so easy."

What was this tempest that thundered over her? This abyss that yawned in front of her?

LeCour crossed the room and paused at the door. "It'll be easy," he said with finality.

Sarah frowned at him. His enchanting smile had turned to wolves teeth. His chocolate eyes were dark pits of quicksand.

The door shut.

Five minutes later Andy limped into the cabin. "Ma, I don't like that man."

Sarah stood stone-like, holding the snapshot. "Who, Son?" she asked numbly.

"That Mr. LeCour. When I came home he was climbin' the bluff over by the gap. And he had a gun. What's he gonna shoot, Ma?"

Sarah whirled. "A gun? He had a gun?"

"Yes, Ma. He didn't see me. He was workin' his way up bein' real careful to stay behind bushes. What's he doin', Ma?"

Phil with a gun. Heading toward the gap. Going after Jake!

Hurriedly she went to the sideboard and cut Andy a thick slice of bread. Her hands shook as she dribbled apple preserves on both the bread and the table.

She leaned down and looked Andy in the eye. "Andy, I want you to stay right here. Don't go out of the cabin. Promise me, Andy."

"Yes, Ma. But what—"

"I can't explain. I have to find your pa. Just do as I say."

She ran from the cabin and was well on the path to the bluff when she remembered the snapshot lying on the table. Andy would see it as he ate his bread and preserves.

She began to climb, her skirts hindering her efforts. "Jake, Jake," she cried, grasping at bushes to pull herself up.

"What have I done? How could I be so stupid? Jake, Jake, please don't come yet. Don't come."

Her skirts tripped her and she fell. She skinned her elbow and scratched her cheek. Anger gave her strength. "When I get my hands on you, Philip LeCour, I'll—"

She lifted her skirts, twisted them tightly and threw them over one arm. She began her climb once again. The rocks bruised her fingers as she clutched and clung to them, inching upward.

Above her she saw Phil perched at the edge of the bluff. His gun was raised.

Any moment it could be too late. Her heart hammered. Her lungs burned.

Carefully, stealthily, she crawled onto the ledge and stood. A pebble rolled under her foot and clattered down the hillside.

LeCour turned his head. His predatory countenance changed instantly. "Sarah, my love."

She scooped up a small rock and rushed at him. The rock hit him squarely on the side of the head. His eyes rounded in surprise.

Still holding the gun, he lunged at her. "You hit me, Sarah, what's—"

She grabbed a second rock and hit him in the chest. He reached out. His fingertips grasped at her sleeve, tearing the fabric as she broke loose. She sidestepped. Momentum carried him forward. His foot slipped. As he grappled to regain his balance, she shoved him. The gun fired.

"You dirty little—" He faltered, then plunged over the edge of the bluff.

Sarah fell to her knees, fearful of what she would see. Her breath came in gasps. Her mouth tasted bitter. Phil lay at the bottom, groaning and gripping one leg.

Sarah struggled against her tangled skirts and stood. She breathed deeply. "It's over. At last it's over." The breeze cooled and steadied her. Her skirts fanned and rippled gently.

Jake galloped to the base of the bluff as Sarah lifted a shaky arm in greeting.

He reined in and tipped his hat. "Afternoon, LeCour." Then he raised his face to the precipice where Sarah watched. He called, "Seems to me your dancin' is a little rough. You broke this man's leg."

An hysterical laugh caught in Sarah's throat and became a sob. "Jake, oh Jake, I love you."

Hours later Sarah and Jake sat before the fire. Andy was asleep in the loft. Jake unlaced his boots and stretched his feet on the fender of the stove.

"Sure good to be home again." His gaze lingered on Sarah's face. "Guess we pulled apart some this summer. Didn't mean it to happen. Had so much on my mind. That whole valley to survey. Some of it so steep I had to slope chain. Settlers chafin' at the bit to sink a plow in. All those patents on the land. Place's gettin' downright crowded."

"You worked hard."

"Got it done though. Had to be gone a lot."

"I didn't mind."

"Yes, you did. I could tell. Couldn't seem to do anythin' about it. Then every time I came home I opened my mouth and yelled at you."

"Yelled?"

"Well, disagreed. Seems like a long time since our opinions had anything to do with one another."

He got up, selected an apple from a bowl and polished it on his pant leg. "...like the Ruehl younguns. I been thinkin'. That Ralphie's a good enough boy. Deserves a chance. Thought maybe I'd offer to let him apprentice to me. Surveyin's hard work but it beats stealin' chickens." He grinned sideways at her.

A kindly warmth enveloped Sarah. Her eyes misted and her voice turned husky. "Thank you, Jake. Ralphie will work hard. I know he will."

Jake opened his pocket knife and tested the blade with his thumb. "'Course, that won't solve Salvia's problem." He shook his head. "Some women sure can get themselves into scrapes."

Sarah waited. Two bright spots appeared on her cheeks.

Jake's knife bit the apple skin. The peeling spiraled into his lap as he turned it around and around. He offered Sarah a slice speared on the tip of his knife.

"Fella once told me," he said leisurely, "best way to test a woman's love is to go away for a spell and see what happens."

Sarah's eyes flickered over his face. She said nothing.

Jake bit into the apple. "Sheriff says LeCour's wanted in Paisley for extortion."

"Ummm." Sarah accepted another slice of apple.

Jake chewed thoughtfully. "Just what were you two doin' up there on that bluff together?"

Sarah's eyes turned saucy. "Picking berries."

"Maybe you were pickin' berries, but he was fixin' to pick me off like I was a sittin' duck."

Jake threw the peeling into the fire. Through the open firebox door they watched it writhe and blacken. The fire settled and chuckled to itself.

Jake leaned forward and slapped his knee. "Dad gum it, Sarah, next time you wanta toss a fella over a cliff, hold off a little. I was about to drill him and you spoiled the whole thing."

Sarah banked ashes over the coals while Jake blew out the lamp and shrugged loose from his suspenders. He took Sarah by the hand and drew her close.

"We've got some catchin' up to do," he murmured in her hair.

Sarah reached up and caressed the back of his neck. They were kissing in the darkened room when they heard a pounding on the door.

Jake groped for the lamp, scratched a match and lit the wick. Sarah released the bolt and swung the door wide.

Ralphie Ruehl stood there, swaying slightly, grief twisting his features. "It's Salvia, Mrs. Weatherby. My sister, Salvia. She—she—she drowned herself down by the log boom. Her and Israel. They're both—"

Sarah pulled the boy into her arms and held him hard against her chest. She tried to think of comforting words, but only groans issued from her lips.

Then she noticed Mrs. Ruehl standing in the path. Lamplight shining through the open doorway reflected on the woman's glittering eyes. The deep creases in her face looked like knife cuts. She held the baby dress that Sarah had given Salvia. It fluttered silver-white against the night sky. Her face became an ugly mask as she pulled her hands apart. Sarah heard the ripping sound of the fabric and watched the little dress tear in half.

Mrs. Ruehl dropped the ragged remnants on the ground and turned away. Sarah stared into the shadows. Then she gently urged Ralphie into the cabin.

"Come sit down, Ralphie," she said. Her voice was cross-stitched with sorrow. "Jake and I want to talk to you."

Chapter Twenty Four
THE DOG-FIGHT

It was dark. A man with a crutch under one arm struggled through the shadows to a large house on a knoll. His crutch scraped the ground as it dragged along the path. Every few steps he glanced over his shoulder.

"Cursed dark," he mumbled. "Can't see. What if somebody's watching? What if somebody's following me?"

At last he reached the back door of the house and knocked. He was yanked indoors.

"How dare you risk coming here." The judge glowered at LeCour.

"I had to go somewhere. They're looking for me."

"What do you mean?"

"The sheriff. They're after me. You've got to hide me."

"Hide you? Are you crazy? What have you done to yourself?"

"I drew a bead on Weatherby and the missus pushed me over a cliff. Hurt my ankle. Doc bound it up and I sneaked out before—"

"You fool! You went too far. I never told you to go after Weatherby."

LeCour shifted his weight. He winced. "I had my reasons. How was I to know she'd catch on to me? No female ever did before."

"Well, you've failed. You're no use to me now. Get out."

LeCour's eyes hardened. "Just a minute, Judge. You forgot something. I haven't got my pay. I demand my wages."

Blotches appeared on Featherstone's face. The fat blobs on his cheeks shook as he leaned over LeCour. "You didn't finish the job. I promised you a reward when you finished. All you did was incriminate yourself. Now get out."

The two men stood eye to eye. LeCour braced his feet.

"I'm not going without my pay. You owe me."

The judge's heavy hand gripped his shoulder. "You're going out this door, LeCour. I can't afford to have somebody see you here. I let nothing endanger my reputation. Remember? So you had a little hard luck. Sorry, friend. It's no concern of mine."

LeCour felt Featherstone's fingers dig viciously into his flesh. The judge was turning him out. The judge never intended to pay. This was his thanks, insult upon insult, trickery and betrayal.

The pain in LeCour's ankle knifed up his leg. He cursed the pain and then the judge. He licked his lips. "You'll pay, Judge. I'll see to it. Nobody shunts me off like this. Not even you."

He raised his fist and shook it.

Suddenly Featherstone opened the door. He snatched the crutch and wrenched it from LeCour's hand. It clattered on the flagstone walkway beyond the door.

"Go after your crutch, LeCour. You're a man who needs such things. You can't lean on me any more."

The judge gave him a push. LeCour swayed and groped for balance. He hobbled outside and stumbled over the crutch. As he struggled to pick it up the door slammed behind him.

Darkness closed around him. With it came the image of Sarah's eyes, full of anger and hurt. He had lost her...lost her for good.

For a moment defeat shafted his heart. But the immediate pain of his throbbing ankle sharpened his urge to strike back at the judge. He would never forget the hate smoldering in Featherstone's eyes. He would show him. Nobody walked on Philip LeCour like that.

He skulked away, glancing furtively at shifting shadows. An idea began to take shape. "Ha," he muttered. "That'd fix him. Fix him good."

Panting, Featherstone leaned against the closed door.

"Fool. Blasted fool." He shook his head, trying to erase the image of LeCour's defiant fist. "Might have known that dandy would botch it. I'll get that woman myself. One of these days...I'll get her."

Chapter Twenty Five
THE DEBATE

Sarah stood at the stove stirring cornmeal mush. She glanced toward the table where Jake and Ralphie leaned over survey documents. The lamplight of early morning shone on their hair and cast shadow images of Ralphie's long lashes on his cheeks. It had been two weeks since Ralphie came to live with them.

Sarah listened as Jake explained surveying terms to Ralphie, "Now when I say cadastral, I mean..."

Sarah turned back to the stove. She arranged bacon in the iron skillet.

Behind her, Jake said, "By the time you're a deputy surveyor, you'll wonder how we ever got along with these clumsy chains. Of course, I'm used to 'em. I have an idea they'll still call it chainin' after everybody's switched to the new steel tapes. Old terms hang on. Now, here's another thing you should keep in mind..."

Sarah went to the spring house for milk and butter. When she returned she heard Jake say, "Some fellows don't think it matters a whit, but I always measure to the center of the tree. Seems to me that's the only way to do it. That's how I measured our witness tree."

Sarah poked at the coals in the stove and shoved in the last stick from the woodbox.

Andy limped into the house. "Guess what I saw by the woodpile? A little cottontail. S'pose he's lookin' for a winter home? Can I catch him for a pet, Pa?"

Jake's expression changed. "You're almost late for breakfast, Son. Your ma needs the woodbox filled and you're out there chasin' a rabbit."

The excitement on Andy's face subsided. "I'm sorry, Pa. Guess I just forgot, thinkin' about that cottontail."

Ralphie scraped his chair backwards and stood. "I'll get

the wood."

Jake's voice boomed in the small room. "No. Andy brings the wood in."

"Yes, Pa." Andy responded meekly.

Sarah stirred the mush mechanically and shot a disapproving glance at Jake. She sliced bread and drained the bacon. As she watched Andy her indignation grew.

Andy struggled. He panted. He stumbled once and almost fell. His task completed at last, he brushed wood chips from his arms.

Sarah's back was turned when Jake smiled and said quietly, "Good job, Son."

Sarah didn't hear Jake's affirmation. She jabbed another stick of wood into the fire box and lifted the tin dishpan onto the stove. The dishwater would be steaming hot when breakfast was over. Her thoughts already simmered. It seemed to Sarah that Jake enjoyed pushing Andy to the limit. Why else would he be so hard on him?

After both boys had gone to school Sarah noticed Jake standing beside the witness tree. Maybe, if she tried now, she could get Jake to understand how she felt about Andy. And the fact that he was an only child. She wanted to talk about Ralphie too. It might be a good idea to start with Ralphie. She draped her shawl around her shoulders and joined Jake.

"Just takin' in the view on my own land before I set off again," he said.

Sarah slipped her hand into the crook of his elbow. "I wish Ralphie didn't have to miss so much school when he goes with you," she began.

"Don't let that bother you. He's a smart boy."

"But he needs to learn—"

"I can teach him all the cipherin' he needs to know when we're out in the brush. He's a good speller too. He wrote up the field notes last time we were out."

Sarah traced the tree bark with a forefinger. "Our witness tree," she said, recalling Phil's intention to cut it down.

"It's a fine looking tree."

Jake nodded. "Yep. Healthy and straight. It'll be here another hundred years or so. That is, if folks treat it right and bugs don't get it. Might even sprout up some little ones if the weather fancies it."

"...little ones,..." Sarah murmured. "Jake—" she said tentatively."

"That's my name."

"I wish Andy had a little brother."

Jake's jaw set. "No use havin' another one till you quit spoilin' the first one."

"Jake, I'm serious."

"Well, I am too. You're far too easy on Andy. He's growin' up thinkin' he doesn't have to—"

"But his leg. Surely you can see that—"

Jake's mouth grew rigid. "What I see is you coddlin' him, makin' allowances for him, instead of expectin' him to measure up. He thinks he can use that leg for an excuse."

"But some things are so hard for him."

"Sure they are. Sure they are. And which do you think gives him the most pride? Never tryin' because he might fail or tacklin' somethin' hard and gettin' it done?"

Jake bent to pick up a rock and rolled it between his palms. "I won't have a son that goes through life makin' excuses for doin' nothin."

Sarah sighed. "I don't think you understand my point. I hate to see him get hurt."

"That's the mother in you talkin'. Can't fault you for that. Might help you to pretend you're a hard-bitten old cattle drover sometimes. Best for the boy in the long run." He tossed the rock over the fence. "Anyhow, as for addin' to the family, you're kinda busy with your 'warrin' women' to look after another youngun."

"Warring women! Jake, what a way to talk about the suffrage movement."

"Well, it's the truth, isn't it? You're always havin'

meetins' and thinkin' of ways to jar the menfolk loose."

"And we're gaining too." Eagerness crowded in.

"You'd be surprised, Jake. In fact, I'm having some ladies over tomorrow afternoon to discuss our next project."

"Tomorrow afternoon," he repeated. "Guess I'm leavin' just in time."

He meant only to joke. His eyes sparkled and his lips turned upward. Sarah took affront. She tightened her shawl and walked away.

As she rounded the corner of the cabin she heard Jake slap the trunk of the witness tree and say, "Well, old tree, good thing you can't repeat what you hear."

Sarah slammed the cabin door, rolled up her sleeves and began to mix bread dough. As she punched and kneaded she eased her angered heart.

"I won't let you upset me, Jake Weatherby. 'Warring women', indeed. I'll make you proud of me yet. We'll win this fight. And then...maybe I can forget...how foolish I was to be deceived by Phil and..." A tear fell into the spongy dough. "I hope the sheriff caught him...what if I see him again...I'd rather die first."

The following afternoon a dozen women gathered in Sarah's cabin. Fanny Cantrell took possession of the rocking chair and proudly nursed little Hiram.

Sarah led a lively discussion of plans for a march at the town hall.

Eliza Murdock protested. "I don't think I could do any of that, Sarah. If my husband knew I was in on this he'd forbid me to come here. I-I told him it was a literary meeting."

Sarah answered firmly, "That's just the point Eliza, Our men are content to let us while away our free time, precious little though it is, with pursuits that don't gain anything. They're satisfied as long as we stay on the same old treadmill, going nowhere."

Eliza tried to interrupt. Sarah held up her hand, "Let me

finish, Eliza. We must let them know we intend to break out of the mold they've set for us."

Lottie Hansen spoke up, "I agree with you, Sarah." She shifted her long legs under her skirts. "We bear the babies. We work as hard as the men. We share the sorrows and pains. And we're entitled to the vote."

A spattering of clapping went around the circle of women. Tiny Hortense Adler cleared her throat and twisted her hands in her lap. Her face reddened as everyone turned to look at her. "I think I'd better go home," she whispered. "My husband's right. I wouldn't know who to vote for anyway. I'd have to ask him. Frank says I haven't got the brains to figure it out myself." She kept her eyes downcast and walked softly out the door.

Sarah stood. "That, ladies, is another reason to fight for our freedom to vote. Hortense has as much good sense as the rest of us. She's been badgered by her husband into thinking otherwise. Let's decide. Shall we march on town hall tomorrow evening?"

Fanny Cantrell lifted Hiram to her shoulder and gently patted him. "I say yes," she said. "Besides, I have good news. Mr. Cantrell told me at breakfast that women should be allowed to vote. I know he'll support us. I can guarantee it."

Her face shone. "He even asked my opinion on a city council matter to be discussed tomorrow evening. Think of that, ladies. The mayor asked my opinion."

Sarah's voice rose on the wave of approval that swept the group. "So then, let's make our placards and practice our marching."

When the meeting adjourned and the ladies had gone home, Sarah stoked the fire and stood for a moment listening to the wood crackle. This was the breakthrough she had waited for. Mayor Cantrell held the key. With his backing the town would fall in line.

The teakettle began to sing. A smile played at the corners of Sarah's mouth. At last. Now she could show Jake some real progress. Oh, it would be good to see the pride on Jake's face when he came home.

Chapter Twenty Six
THE DEBACLE

Sarah's suffragettes stood on the steps of the town hall. The setting sun painted gold highlights in their upswept hair. Their dresses were a potpourri of creamy lace and ruchings with bouquets of delicate tatting and embroidery. Each lady held a carefully lettered placard that read: "Women's Suffrage, the Key to Progress-Equality for All Citizens."

Sarah noticed tears in Emma Gurley's eyes. She pressed the young woman's arm. "Don't worry, Emma. We'll be together in there. You can stand by me."

Fanny Cantrell touched her elbow. "We're ready, Sarah."

Sarah looked into each woman's face. "Don't be frightened. Hold your placards high. Show them we're determined. Remember, Mayor Cantrell supports us. And ladies—smile."

Sarah lifted the latch and the women crowded into the vestibule. The odor of stale tobacco lingered in the air.

"Head's up, girls," she whispered. As her hand turned the doorknob to the council chamber her heart pulsed at an alarming rate against the fall of brown silk on her shirtwaist.

Mayor Cantrell heard the door open but didn't bother to turn his head. It was only the deputy returning from the outhouse. Cantrell addressed the council. "You have heard the question, gentlemen. Shall the City of Nugget install another horse trough at the south end of Front Street and extend the boardwalk to accommodate Murphy's Saloon?"

His voice rose with expectation. "Are we ready for the vote?" Civic improvements were always a plus for an incumbent hoping for re-election. "All in favor say—"

At that moment a swishing sound filled the room as a dozen skirts flounced across the oiled oak floor.

Startled, Mayor Cantrell turned. "What is this interrup -" He saw his wife. He hurriedly scanned the placards. A vein in his forehead bulged.

The council members rose. Their heads pivoted, following the line of women circling the room.

Cantrell's neck strained against his celluloid collar. "Ladies, I beg of you—"

The women paid no attention to him. They continued their march around the room. Cantrell's gaze locked on Sarah's face. This was her doing. He might have known she would try something like this.

Sarah paused in front of Cantrell and the procession stopped. Cantrell could hear his own breathing in the suddenly quiet room.

Immediately Sarah's clarion voice rang in his ears, "Sir, we petition this council and pray that you will enter into the record of your business that the town of Nugget, Washington Territory, stands for women's suffrage and urges all other communities to do the same."

Cantrell dragged his gaze from Sarah's face and glanced sideways at his wife. "Fanny, go home," he whispered.

Fanny Cantrell's placard shook. Her face grew pink. "No, Mr. Cantrell. I cannot."

Cantrell eyed his fellow councilmen. Boesley made a fuss of tamping his pipe. Johnson shuffled papers. Silwatch and Dieter pretended interest in a fly crawling on the wall.

Cantrell's best friend, Ernest Southwood, stood hands-in-pockets, while a mischievous grin twitched at his mouth. Southwood cleared his throat. Cantrell heard the beginning of a chuckle. "Maybe we ought to hear the ladies out, Cyrus. Won't hurt nothin'."

Sarah seized the opportunity. Her voice sounded over the buzzing in Cantrell's head. "Sir, perhaps you would like me to repeat—"

"I heard, Mrs. Weatherby. No need to—to repeat." His tongue felt swollen. If Featherstone should walk in this minute...

Cantrell glanced again at the other men. He noted their

149

questioning eyes and shrugging shoulders. He had to take command.

"This is a business meeting, Mrs. Weatherby, we cannot brook intrusion." Even to himself that sounded absurd. Men often brought their grievances before the council. Men, that is, never women.

He tried again, his voice a hoarse bellow. "Mrs. Weatherby, you will please conduct your ladies outside this council chamber at once."

What was the matter with this woman? She had not budged. And Fanny, his own wife, stood there undaunted. Didn't she see how embarrassing this was? He had to get rid of them some way.

Amid the confusion of his thoughts he heard Sarah saying, "...do not intend to leave until we have the desired action by the council."

Desired action by the council! Cantrell's discomfort mounted. He longed to scratch where the sweat trickled between his shoulder blades. He closed his eyes and saw himself teetering between what was right and what would get him re-elected.

And, blast it all, he liked being mayor. He liked the feeling of importance. He was a good mayor. Everybody said so. He swallowed and opened his mouth, but the voice came from the opposite side of the room. Featherstone's voice!

"Well, well, well, what have we here? Ripe plums from the tree, Cantrell?"

Cantrell felt the floorboards vibrate as Featherstone crossed the room. The judge paused beside Sarah and surveyed her with malevolent eyes. "Mrs. Weatherby, you have arrived at a most opportune moment."

Cantrell knew what was coming. His fingertips turned to ice. Featherstone advanced toward him, his footsteps sounding a fateful dirge. His tone began as distant thunder and quickly crescendoed to a roar.

"Clear the room, Cantrell. At once."

Cantrell's throat was clogged. "Deputy," he quavered.

"Escort these ladies to the conference room and book them. Then release them. And Deputy—"

"Yes, Sir?"

"Escort Mrs. Weatherby to the jail."

Featherstone met Cantrell's glance with a satisfied smirk. The mayor sat down abruptly and covered his face with his hands.

Time and space blurred for Sarah. She heard placards drop to the floor, women cry and chairs scrape. Southwood's voice carried above the commotion, "Think for yourself, Cyrus. Think for yourself."

A firm hand closed around Sarah's arm and propelled her down a hallway. A door clanged shut. She found herself standing in a shadowy cubicle gripping cold iron bars.

She had led her ladies into ambush. Too late, she realized Cantrell was Featherstone's lackey. Too late, she realized a man's private opinion might differ from his public image. Too late...

Twenty minutes later the other women were released. Fanny Cantrell clung to her husband's arm, weeping as they went out the door together.

Two of the women peered into Sarah's cell. "Goodbye, dear," they whispered. "Don't worry. We'll tell Jake."

The building quieted. Sarah stood stiff and unyielding. Her heartbeat seemed to synchronize with the tick of the clock in the hallway. She could see a portion of the council chamber where her placard still lay on the floor. Through the open door of the sheriff's office she glimpsed the pot-bellied stove. From the spout of a granite coffeepot perched on top rose aromatic steam.

Coffee. Hot, strong coffee. She would die before she asked for some.

The deputy sauntered down the hall, his shoes scuffing the floor. "You want anythin', Mrs. Weatherby?"

Sarah shook her head.

The deputy scratched under his collar. "You need somethin', just rattle the bars. That's what they all do." His gaze shifted to the wall above her head. "Never had a woman prisoner before." He shuffled away, leaving the hall door ajar.

Just rattle the bars, indeed. She was in jail. In jail! Jake would come. And then she remembered. Jake was off running a survey line, tracking the wilderness.

And Andy? Lil had tucked him into bed by now. Sarah envisioned Lil singing to him an Indian lullaby. They would not know where she was. Thank goodness, they would not know.

The dark, silent hours slid by. Sarah eased onto the bench at the back of the cell and pulled a rough woolen blanket over her.

Her eyes narrowed at the beam of light shining through the hall door. "I'm right. I know I'm right. I'll never give up. Never," she whispered.

She turned her face into the dirty straw tick so the deputy would not hear her crying.

Chapter Twenty Seven
THE DAY OF RECKONING

Every seat in the courtroom was taken. Banker and apprentice, cattle drover and haberdasher, stood shoulder to shoulder against the walls. The grime-streaked windows cast a sickly yellow sheen over their faces.

Sarah searched the crowd. Had her friends come to support her? Or did they mingle with the ones who came to sneer and ogle, pretending they had never shared her dream?

A low buzz rose and fell among the spectators. Sarah heard their whisperings. Among the press of bodies she saw brows being mopped with handkerchiefs and elbows prodding ribs. Before her eyes they blurred into a faceless mass.

Her hands trembled in her lap. Her shoulders slumped. Since her arrest, anxiety and self-incrimination had exhausted her. All her hopes and ambitions had come to nothing. What had Big Lil said? "...if you are right others will follow." Well, Lil was wrong. Abigail Duniway was wrong too. It had been foolish to believe in her, to hope. There was nothing to be gained, now, or ever—ever again.

Sarah could hardly swallow. Her throat tightened as she glanced at Jake from under her lashes. A messenger had been sent to find him. He cut short his surveying expedition and galloped home. Before her arrest they had begun to mend the breach that Phil had caused. Now she had torn it open, a jagged wound that would never heal.

She longed to have him reach out and squeeze her hand. But she knew he wouldn't. If she could just press her face against his chest and feel his arms around her. Would he ever do that again? Would he ever want to?

A murmur rippled through the crowd. Sarah jumped as the judge banged his gavel. His voice sliced into the stuffy room, scattering a swarm of flies that circled the ceiling.

"Will the defendant please rise."

Sarah obeyed, blinking her eyes and fighting dizziness.

"...Disrupting our peaceful community, exploiting its womenfolk..."

Who was this awful person described by his droning voice?

"...inciting to riot, destroying..."

The accusations hit like hammer blows upon her consciousness.

"No! No! That's not true!" Had she spoken?

Someone hissed in her ear, "Be quiet, Sarah. For once in your life be quiet."

Sarah's head pounded. The memory of the day she sat in the Judge's private chamber flitted across her mind. His voice oozed sweetness then. There was no honey in his tone now.

"...I therefore, as Judge of this Circuit Court in the Territory of Washington, do sentence you..."

The room began to pitch and sway. Someone's arm held Sarah steady. She tried to concentrate on the judge's face. His eyes leered at her and from the dark hole of his open mouth poured ominous words.

"...You will be allowed to return home in the custody of your husband to set your affairs in order. On the morrow at seven a.m. a conveyance will arrive to transport you to the county jail at Stone Mountain. There you will remain until such time as deemed advisable by this court for the termination of your sentence. This court is now adjourned."

He banged the gavel.

Sarah heard the gasps that swept over the crowd. Flutterings of breath long held, hands made suddenly busy, murmurings and oaths, surged and receded among the people. Never in the history of Nugget had a woman been so shamed.

As one body the assembly rushed toward the door. Jake's hand gripped Sarah's arm. He led with his shoulder, pressing away from the turmoil.

Sarah felt a tug at her sleeve.

"Jist wanted to see what a jailhouse female feels like."

The toothless face split into a hideous grin. Claw-like hands grabbed the fabric of her dress. "Lookie here, folks. Pretty fancy for a jailhouse female."

Other hands reached out, pulling at her clothes, pinching and probing.

"Feels like a woman, don't it?"

"Reckon she'll wear different clothes once she gets behind bars?"

In the midst of grasping hands and mocking faces Jake's voice exploded. Suddenly his fists and feet were everywhere, lashing out and scattering her tormentors.

"Get away, you jackals!" he yelled.

Sarah caught sight of his face. In all their years of marriage she had never seen such fury rage in his features. The contempt in his eyes and the defiance in his jaw sent a bolt of fear through her.

The hecklers shrank away, their eyes wide, their mouths agape. Sarah heard Jake whisper, "Quick. Through the door. Then run for the buggy."

She felt the warmth of his cheek near hers. Was there a chance he still cared? A sob rose in her throat. Then they were out of the building, running hard with the mocking crowd behind them.

Judge Featherstone tried not to snicker as he watched the people flow from the courtroom. He knew they were stunned. Sarah's sentence effected the shock he had planned. The fact that she had a son was all the better. He had struck a blow where a woman would feel it the most. She would be separated from Andy. No other woman would so much as let out a peep lest she suffer the same fate. This would squash the woman's suffrage movement in Washington Territory for good.

A corner of his mouth twitched with pleasure. The courtroom ruffians he hired had done a good job.

The last of the crowd jostled out the door while the judge unfastened his robe. As evening shadows descended cool air eddied in the darkening recesses of the room.

Something stirred in a far corner. The judge paid no attention. Secure in his victory, he retired to his chamber.

He poured a glass of whiskey and stood at the window smiling. Darkness seeped into the streets. No need to light the lamp. The cloak of night suited him fine. He had put Sarah out of the way himself. Didn't need that fool LeCour after all. Or that jelly-hearted hunchback.

The floor creaked behind him. He turned. The shaft of a knife pierced the center of his chest. His limbs bent at the joints. His body crumpled, piling upon itself like a marionette and forming an immense heap on the floor.

A hunched man in ragged clothes stood over him. "Somebody had to stop ya, Boss," he said. He stooped and pinned a note to the judge's chest. Barely discernible in the fading light, it read:" A reward fitly earned."

The hunchback tiptoed from the room, latched the door and blended with the shadows in the corridor.

Sarah and Jake rode the gauntlet of Front Street. She sat bowed, staring at her hands. The sun slid behind the trees, pulling a grey cloud blanket over its head. Rain sprinkles pocked the dusty street. Townsfolk stood in gossip-clusters under the shelter of eaves. A drunk emerged from the saloon, bringing tinkling music and the glare of lamplight with him. He jeered as they passed.

Jake stared straight ahead, contemplating Lady's hip bones. Sarah wished he would say something, anything, even scolding words. It was beyond hope that he would comfort her. She could not expect that ever again. He had warned her and she had ignored him.

They waited while a freight wagon loaded with barrels crossed in front of them. At last they were free of the town. Their cabin and the witness tree stood in the dusk like a charcoal drawing.

"Where is he?" Sarah asked, not daring to look up.

"Who?" Jake's voice was wooden.

"Andy."

"Big Lil's."

She licked her lips. "Does—does he know?"

"Nope."

"And—and Ralphie?"

"Left him with the crew." Jake's tone dismissed further exchange of words.

They turned into the lane. Jake pulled up by the cabin. "You go on in. I'll fetch Andy."

Sarah climbed down and stood beside the buggy. Their eyes held for a moment.

"Didn't turn out like you planned, did it?" he said. He looked away, clucked to Lady and slapped the reins.

Sarah stood on the doorstep watching the buggy jostle down the narrow track that led to Lil's cabin. She looked over the fields, tracing the path to the gap. Home. When would she see it again?

Her eyes followed the curve of the road back to Nugget. It was then that she saw the glow and the smoke billow over the housetops.

"Mill's on fire," she said. "Mill's on fire."

Chapter Twenty Eight
THE DETOUR

Sarah looked anxiously toward Lil's cabin. Out of the darkness she heard Jake yell, "Git up, you old hoss." Then the buggy emerged, rocking from side to side as Jake leaned forward slapping the reins. Andy's small white face appeared beside him. The buggy skidded to a stop.

Jake jumped down and yelled to Sarah, "Unhitch for me." He raced to the barn.

Sarah locked Lady in the corral as Jake saddled Moses and galloped off to fight the fire. Then she and Andy stood together watching the flames rise above the rooftops of Nugget. She put her arm around him and searched for words. How could she tell him she had been sentenced to jail?

"Andy?"

"Yes, Ma?"

"I have something to—er—you must—never mind."

No, she could not say it. And she was so tired...so tired...

They went into the cabin. Crooning soft endearments, she tucked him into his loft bed. She crossed the kitchen, pushed aside the curtain and lay down on her quilted coverlet.

Her fingers stroked the stitching lines. It was a wedding present from her ma. She remembered well her mother's wishes for a happy marriage.

A happy marriage? She had destroyed it. What man wanted a wife who was hauled into court, shamed before the whole town and jailed? And what man would endure whispers and accusations? She could hear the gossips now, their fingers pointing: "That's the woman who stirred up the whole town. Got herself put away in the jailhouse." No, she couldn't expect Jake to live with that.

And what would happen to Andy? Sarah rolled onto her side, clutched the quilt and wadded it in her fist. The children would taunt, "Yer ma's in the jailhouse, the jailhouse."

Sarah snatched the edge of the quilt and pulled it over her like a shield against the despair that assaulted her. As she agonized a sudden idea broke through her despondency. After a moment she whispered, "It's the only way."

She quickly gathered some things into her portmanteau. Hurrying, she ran to the barn, hitched Lady to the buggy and drove to the doorstep. "Andy," she called softly. She used precious time coaxing him down the ladder from the loft. As she set him in a chair he whimpered.

"Shh, Andy. Just be still."

From a high shelf she took down a bottle of laudanum, poured a few drops into a dish and mixed it with water and honey.

"Wake up, Andy. Hold your head up. That's a good boy. Ma has something for you."

She lifted the sleepy boy to a sitting position and shook him gently. "Here, Son. Open your mouth. Swallow this."

"Ma? What? I wanna go back to—"

"Hush, Andy. Let me help you get your clothes on. Hold out your arms."

"But, Ma, it's dark. I'm sleepy. I—"

"Yes, I know, Andy. In a little while you can sleep all you want. But first you must help me. There now."

With fingers flying she buttoned his clothes. She laced his boots and half-carried the stumbling boy to the buggy. As she covered him with a blanket she murmured, "Sleep now, Andy. Just go to sleep."

She rushed back into the cabin. Bending over a lighted candle stub, she scrawled a note to Jake: "Please don't try to find me. I've taken Andy...so sorry..."

The knot in her throat tightened. She wiped her tear-streaked face with a corner of her cloak, propped the note beside the salt shaker and blew out the candle.

She paused a moment on the doorstep. Home. She might never see it again.

In the buggy Sarah touched Andy's shoulder. "Andy?" She leaned closely and listened to his gentle snoring, then flicked the reins over Lady's back.

Sarah guided the horse over the embankment and onto the same overgrown trail she had used the night she carried the leaflets to the meeting house. Closer to the fire now, she heard the crack and roar of the flames as they mingled with the shouts of the men.

They formed a bucket brigade from the stream that flowed into the public horse trough. Sarah saw their legs scissor back and forth, silhouetted against the flames. Jake was among them—somewhere. It gave her a strange empty feeling to know she was already set apart, an outsider looking on.

As the buckets passed from hand to hand in a continuous chain, steam billowed where water splashed on glowing timbers. Horses snorted and whinnied in terror. Above the commotion the thundering fire devoured the mill.

Sarah urged Lady forward. Smoke stung her nostrils. Cinders and soot drifted over her path. Glowing embers winked and floated in the grass. They sizzled, burned out and left tiny spirals of smoke jetting into the air.

Lady nickered and trembled.

"Easy, Lady, easy." Sarah's fingers tightened on the reins. "We'll soon be past." She glanced at Andy, making sure his face was covered by the blanket.

From the corner of her eye she caught a sudden movement. A man with an awkward shambling gait darted in front of the buggy. Lady shied.

Sarah screamed, "Watch out!"

The man grabbed Lady's bridle and hung on.

"Stop! Stop that! Who are you?" Sarah demanded. "Get away from my horse."

Lady tossed her head. The buggy jerked and swayed. The man edged along Lady's quivering flank, got hold of the buggy and lifted his foot onto the step. At that moment the roof of the planing shed collapsed, sending leaping flames into the sky. Showers of sparks illuminated the area.

Sarah stared into the man's soot-streaked face. "Phil! What are you doing here? Get away from me. No, no, go away."

She pushed at him. He brushed her hands aside, climbed in and hauled a large container onto the seat.

"Let's get out of here," he said.

Sarah's panic erupted in anger. "What are you doing? Get out of my buggy."

The shooting flames played strange lights across his face. Sarah saw the changing expressions in his eyes. She watched in horror as the familiar devilish grin spread over his mouth.

"Looks like we're both doing the same thing, Sarah," he said. "Running away. You running from Jake? Might as well go together, the way I see it."

"What's in that can?"

"Never mind the can."

"It's kerosene, isn't it? It was you. You set the fire. Get out of my buggy. Get out!"

She pushed at him again. He seized her wrist. His other hand closed over her fingers that held the reins. He forced her arm up and down. "Get up, Lady," he said.

The buggy moved.

Sarah kicked at him. "You awful man. How could you do this to me?"

He held her arm with punishing fingers. "Settle down," he ordered. "You want me to tip the kid over the side?"

They moved into the shadows, leaving the fire behind.

"Don't you dare touch Andy. Don't you dare." Sarah's voice cracked.

"How come he's sleeping?"

"He's—he's just tired—that's all."

"You're a rotten liar, Sarah. No kid could sleep through all this."

Sarah did not answer. His grip pinched her arm. The

161

buggy jolted around a corner. The firelight faded.

"Where are you taking me?" she asked.

"What do you mean?" he shot back. "You're the one who started this trip. I just happened to come along—conveniently."

"Conveniently. That's how it always is with you, Phil. Taking a free ride at somebody else's expense."

"Hasn't cost you anything yet, my pretty one."

"Don't call me your pretty one."

She knew he was laughing silently. He spoke softly in her ear, "I might even have saved you from a nasty accident when that naughty man ran out in front of your buggy."

Sarah turned from him. A loathing for him pervaded her senses. Branches brushed against the buggy. The last traces of smoke thinned and wafted away. The trail narrowed. Tree boughs interlaced over the road.

"Right peaceful, isn't it?" LeCour spoke into the silence. His grip on her arm loosened. The hand enclosing hers relaxed.

Sarah took a deep breath and steadied her voice. "I—I need to go into the bushes. Can't we stop?"

"The bushes, eh? Well now, I suppose we could stop for just a minute. I'll ditch this can of kerosene at the same time."

The buggy halted. Sarah hesitated.

"You first, my dear," he said.

A sudden premonition jolted Sarah. What if he ran away with the buggy?"

LeCour echoed her thoughts. "Seems like we don't trust each other. Tell you what. We'll both get out at the same time."

Sarah heard the slap of leather as he looped the reins around the hand brake. They stood up. The buggy bounced as they stepped to the ground. Sarah groped in the darkness, her outstretched hand feeling for the bushes. On the other side of the buggy she heard him tramping among the trees.

She reached down. Her fingers scrabbled over the ground. She grasped a rock—a stick—another stick. She tossed one, then another into the bushes, imitating the rustling sound of someone passing through.

Lifting her skirts, she ran back and lunged for the buggy. She climbed in and fumbled with the reins. She heard LeCour approaching on the other side. The buggy swayed as his foot balanced on the step.

"Get up, Lady," Sarah yelled. She slapped the reins smartly. "Get up."

The buggy jerked forward. Sarah heard LeCour scuffling in the dirt.

"Hey, hold on. You double-crossing female. Hold on."

Sarah slapped the reins again. "Go, Lady, go!" She braced her feet and peered desperately into the darkness.

Behind her LeCour yelled curses and threw rocks at the buggy. His feet pounded the ground as he lumbered after her.

The buggy grazed a tree. It careened over a rock then bounced through a washout. The road angled steeply downward. The moon lifted over the trees and Sarah glimpsed the river, a silver ribbon winding far below. She could see the road. Its dim grey outline led to the water.

Lady settled into a trot. Sarah hazarded a look backward. There was no sign of LeCour. She leaned against the seat and sighed with thankfulness.

Now, to plan a new life somewhere. She put her hand on the seat to pat her reticule. She still had a nice sum remaining from her teaching money. It would be enough until she could—

The reticule was gone! Panic stung her. Phil had likely discarded it and stashed the money in his pocket. Now what would she do?

Chapter Twenty Nine
THE DILEMMA

Just before dawn Andy raised his head. "Ma?"

"Yes, Son?"

"What're we doin'?"

"Why, we're going to Three Corners." Was her voice too bright?

"What for?"

How could she tell him? "Oh—well, you'll see when we get there."

"It's still dark, Ma." His words were slurred.

"I know, Son."

"Ma?"

"Yes, Andy."

"The buggy keeps bumpin' my ear."

"Then lean on me for a while." She helped him sit up and gathered him close to her side.

"I feel so...sleepy, Ma..."

"It'll pass, Andy."

"Where's Pa? Is he comin' too?" The question jolted Sarah. She might have known he would ask about Jake.

"Well, no—not just yet, he—" She watched Andy's eyelids droop. "Just sleep a little longer, Son. That's my boy. Sleep a little longer."

It was early morning when the two arrived at Three Corners. Sarah faced straight forward, her mouth a grim line. She quickly located the livery stable, set the hand brake and turned to Andy, "You stay here while I talk to the proprietor."

She knocked on the door of the fly-speckled office. The owner poked his head out, wiping at a brown stain that dribbled from a corner of his mouth. He reeked of horse manure and sweat.

Sarah swallowed hard and avoided staring at his dirty broadcloth suit. "Are you open for business?" she inquired.

"You wanna rent a hoss?"

"No Sir, I'd like to sell this horse and buggy."

She heard Andy jump from the buggy and hurry to her side. "Ma. Ma. We can't sell Lady. We can't, Ma."

"Hush, Andy." Sarah pulled him to her. Her hand caressed his cheek. "Just hush."

She turned back to the stable owner. Her breath came raggedly. "I want $25 for the horse and $45 for the buggy."

"Well, ma'am." He lifted his hat and scratched in his greasy hair. "They ain't worth more'n half that." He turned and spit into the straw at the stable entrance.

Sarah lifted her chin. "I won't take a penny less. You can see they've been well taken care of."

The man squinted at her and wiped his mouth with the back of his hand. He shrugged. "All right, ma'am. It's a sale. Cash?"

"Of course."

"But, Ma—"

Sarah's arm tightened around Andy's shoulders. "Hush, Andy."

The man counted the money into her hand, looking slyly at her face.

Sarah's eyes were stern. "You shorted me two dollars."

The man grinned, exposing broken teeth. He dug into his pocket and handed her the rest.

Sarah wanted to lay her cheek next to Lady's soft muzzle and whisper, "Goodbye, old friend." Instead she hauled the portmanteau from the buggy, took Andy by the arm and said crisply, "Good day, sir."

As they walked toward the stage depot merchants shook rugs and swept the boardwalk. They paused to stare at the disconsolate woman and the crying boy.

"Poor child," someone said.

"S'pose he just had a beatin'?"

"The both of 'em runnin' away from somethin' looks to me."

Sarah avoided their curious stares and raised her chin a notch. At the stage depot she settled Andy on a bench while she studied the notices pinned to the wall. She ignored the ones curled at the edges and smudged with grime. The crisp, newer entries caught her attention:

City Assay Office   Drayage anywhere
work solicited in all branches   per yard or barrel
of assaying and analysis
201 Fergus St.

And then she saw it, just above her head:
Town of Tanner Flats soliciting teacher
15 scholars guaranteed
Terms: $45 per month
Duties include cleaning schoolhouse
and building fire each day.

Her thoughts raced. A teacher! Of course. But married women with little boys weren't allowed to teach. So. What if she told them Andy was her—her nephew? She fingered her wedding band. Oh, it was unthinkable...and yet...It was the only way. She slipped the ring into her pocket and felt a tug at her skirt.

"Ma? Why'd we have to sell Lady?"

Sarah glanced down at Andy. The angle of his jaw, so like Jake's sent a stitch through her and she had to look away.

"I can't explain it right now, Andy. Please trust me. We're going to Tanner Flats. You can go to school there. We'll—you—you'll like it there," she finished weakly.

"Where's Tanner Flats, Ma?"

Sarah's shoulders drooped. "I don't know."

When the stage stopped on Tanner Flat's Front Street they were numb with fatigue.

Andy clung to Sarah's arm as she looked around. From

the river bordering the road a mist rose that settled between ramshackle houses. A man sauntered through the swinging doors of a saloon, wafting the tinkling strains of "De Camptown Races," into the evening air.

Sarah noticed the general store and blacksmith shop. They leaned slightly, like two brothers in conversation. Beside a vacant lot of dried corn stalks, the church and schoolhouse huddled, a joint statement of man's eternal reach.

The station master directed Sarah to a boarding house. After they ate a supper of watery cabbage soup and corn bread the grim-faced woman who ran the boarding house frowned and said, "I'll show you to your room now so's I won't have to be bothered with it later on." She opened the door at the head of the stairs.

Sarah surveyed the faded wallpaper, the worn carpet and smoked lamp chimney. The room was permeated with the smell of many cabbage soup suppers.

"Thank you," Sarah said, wishing the proprietress would quit staring.

The woman's feet were planted wide apart. She did not move. Sarah felt ire rise in her throat. "You must be very busy. We won't need anything else."

The proprietress's mouth formed an inaudible "Humph." She raised her ample bosom and said, "Breakfast at six-thirty and I don't wait for late risers."

With a final scorching look she stepped out and closed the squeaking door behind her.

"Ma, what are we doin' here? I don't like it. It stinks in here. I want to go home."

Sarah didn't answer. She settled on the bed, carefully avoiding a stain on the coverlet. Her fingers explored the stabbing pain in her temples. She peered through the greasy window pane as the sun slipped beyond the hills. A bright band rimming the horizon tinged the buildings a dirty yellow.

Sarah was reminded, in wistful comparison, of the sunsets at home. The leaves of the poplar tree in the corner of the yard would be brushed with dappled gold. Would Jake remember to water that tree? If she were home right now she'd be...

Her breath caught in her throat. She had no home. She was a spinster school teacher with a nephew named Andy and...

"Andy," she began, "I'm going to apply for a job as a school teacher and I need your help. You see,..."

When she finished Andy's eyes were round with bewilderment and fear. His lips trembled. "Why, Ma? Why should I call you Auntie Sarah? You're my ma. Why should we be different than we are?"

"Please try to understand, Andy. Please trust me."

"But I don't understand. I miss Pa. I'm scared. We can go home," he pleaded. "I know we can."

"No, Andy. We can't. Not—just yet."

"But I love Pa." Andy's small fists clenched. "You don't want Pa to find us, do you?"

He covered his face with his hands as tears ran between his fingers.

Sarah pulled him to her chest and stroked his hair. She helped him into bed. While he slept she sat at the small table by the window and stared at her reflection in the glass.

There was no going back. Andy was young. He would get used to it, even forget after a while. But what about herself? For the rest of her life she would be haunted. Should she have stayed at Nugget and submitted to the punishment, the mockery, the disgrace?

No. Surely Jake would be relieved to find her gone. Surely he couldn't love her now. He would realize it was best for Andy.

Sarah hugged herself and rocked from side to side.

After a while she blew out the lamp, lay her head on her arms and dozed. She dreamed a great crowd of people were chasing her. Jake and Phil were in the lead, throwing rocks at her. Together they yelled, "That'll teach her."

The scene changed. She was standing before the president of the Tanner Flats school board. He was a man seven feet tall with large yellow teeth. "You sure that's your nephew, ma'am. You trying to pull something over on me?"

She struggled awake, her numb arms prickling. "No. No. Please believe me. Please..."

She raised her head. Outside the window the moon's silver gleam softened the harsh angles of rough boards and broken gates. She undressed, folded her clothes on the chair and slipped into bed. A faraway coyote yipped. His plaintive voice and mournful song echoed her own thoughts and feelings.

Chapter Thirty
THE DISAPPOINTMENT

The chairman of the Tanner Flats school board was not seven feet tall with large yellow teeth. He was a short, rotund man, his features bird-like, his manner precise.

Seated across the table from him, Sarah explained, "I truly need employment, Mr. McCary. I am a teacher. However, I lost my certificate in a fire." That was true, wasn't it? It was irretrievably lost along with her reticule somewhere in the woods beyond Nugget's burned-out mill.

McCary's robin's-breast chest rose and fell as he peered at her over his glasses. "Unfortunate. Most unfortunate. But in Tanner Flats we are victims of circumstance too. Our last teacher decided to get married. Had to let her go."

"Yes," Sarah said. "Of course."

"Tell you what, Miss Weatherby. You show up Monday morning, get the fire going and you got yourself a job."

Sarah rose. "Thank you, Mr. McCary. I do appreciate it."

The small man hopped to his feet. "Er—your nephew. How old is he?

"Andy is eight years old. He's a bright boy, he—"

"Good, good," he said, looking down his beak of a nose. "That makes sixteen for the school. Excellent. Excellent. Now you'll need a place to live. Old Mrs. Cranshaw's boarding house is no place for a teacher." He cocked his head to one side. "Tell you what I have a house for rent. Just the thing for you and your nephew. Let you have it for ten dollars a month."

Sarah tried to look demure. "I'm sorry, Mr. McCary. That's a bit more than I can afford. I'll have to look elsewhere."

"Nonsense, nonsense. Lady like you don't want to traipse all over town. Let you have it for eight."

Sarah's eyes did not flicker. Remembering the dilapidated appearance of the houses on Front Street, she countered,

"Five."

McCary's mouth opened and closed. He blinked. "Five, it is. I'll get the key and show it to you."

It was a five dollar house. A temperamental cook stove, a bench and a table adorned the kitchen. Two straw-tick cots sagged in a lean-to room at the back. The garish wallpaper was streaked where the roof leaked.

"Right cozy, don't you think?" McCary said, flapping his arms.

"Oh, yes," Sarah answered automatically. But her heart wrenched at thoughts of home where sunbeams played on her braided rug and the doors of the oak pie-safe reflected the flickering firelight.

Monday morning Sarah stood before the rickety table that served as a teacher's desk. She smiled at the rows of children seated on long rough-cut benches.

"Boys and girls, we live in an exciting world. Who can tell me what children in Lapland are doing on a day like today?" And later, "Did you know that right this very minute it's bed-time in Prussia. And when we are headed for bed the Prussians are beginning a new day."

The children's eyes shone. They listened intently. Sarah was different from previous teachers.

On Tuesday Sarah began, "Let's talk about occupations. Who can tell me what a ballerina does? Edward, if you were to open an oculist shop what would you need?"

On Wednesday there were repercussions. Willie Bemis came to school with red eyes. "My Pa whupped me," he said. "Said I was showin' off when I tole him little boys in Prussia was goin' to bed when we was gittin' up. My Pa says just because that schoolmarm says it, don't make it so."

Edward was the boy to whom she posed the question about the oculist shop. He told Sarah, "Pa said I'll follow the plow around the field same as him when I'm growed. He says that's my place."

Sarah smiled. "How exciting, Edward, if you were to sell your crops to a far away country some day." She saw a spark of light return to his eyes.

"Do you really think I could, Miss Weatherby?"

Twelve year old Lucy Hammel showed leadership abilities and an artistic flair. After recess on Thursday Sarah suggested, "When you're a grown-up, Lucy, you might think about opening a millinery shop."

Friday morning Sarah received a written reply from Lucy's mother, "Pleas do not put sich hie falutin idears in Lucy's head," read the note.

The school board called a meeting for Saturday morning.

"Miss Weatherby," said chairman McCary. "We are somewhat disconcerted at your methods. We hired you to teach our younguns reading, writing and arithmetic. You are straying considerably from your calling. May I remind you of a teacher's true vocation."

Sarah swallowed her exasperation. "Mr. McCary, I intend to blend interesting facts about our world with the children's basic studies. In this way they will retain the knowledge and be able to use it when they are grown."

McCary bobbed his head. He pointed his beaked nose at her. "Just the same. We didn't ask for fancy teaching. We want our younguns to learn the 'three Rs'. That's enough."

Sarah had so hoped Tanner Flats would be different from Nugget. Now she saw the town was even more provincial.

"...don't teach what we want," McCary was saying, "We can find another teacher who will."

Her disappointment stung. If she could only make them understand.

She tried again, "Your children need to know more of the world than Tanner Flats. They must learn of other cultures, other ideas. When they are adults they will choose from many paths in life and make informed decisions.

With tobacco cud tucked under lip and dirty fingernails hiddenin pockets, one board member made a mental note to ask the parson what Miss Weatherby was talking about. The parson was the only other one he ever heard talk about "decisions in life."

When the door closed on Sarah's rustling skirts, mouths opened simultaneously.

"That woman has more nerve than a gol-durned pig in a poke."

"Too high and mighty fer me. What'd you hire her fer, McCary?"

"What my Ned needs is a two by four aside his bottom, not a outlandish idear in his head."

Sunday afternoon Andy brought a stick from the wood-pile into the house. Sad-eyed and pale, he began to whittle.

"What are you making?" Sarah asked.

"I'm gonna make a horse—like Lady."

Sarah left him alone. Perhaps time would heal what she could not. Surprised by a timid knock at the door, she opened it. There on the doorstep stood a short chubby woman with delft blue eyes.

"Miss Weatherby," she said. "My name's Mary Applegate. You teach my Priscilla at the schoolhouse."

Sarah offered Mary a seat on the kitchen bench, set the kettle to boiling and brewed tea. "Priscilla is making good marks at school, Mary."

"Yes, ma'am." Mary picked nervously at her shawl. "That's sort of what I came to talk about." Her face shone with sincerity. "I think everybody who has a chance to learn ought to take advantage of it, don't you? I don't hold with the way the others say you're putting too fancy ideas in the youngun's heads. I'm so glad Priscilla's learning all those things. She can be a real lady when she grows up. Maybe she can leave this town..."

Mary's soft white hands cradled her teacup. For a moment she was lost in a muse. She turned back to Sarah and spoke rapidly, "I'm right handy with a needle and thread and

I've attended almost fifty birthings too. Most folks call on me for that and—what I mean is—"

She stopped for a breath. Her hand trembled slightly, letting a little of the tea slosh into the saucer. "Priscilla brings home such wonderful stories and she tells me how she's learning all the long words in the spelling books and—"

Mary's eyes pierced Sarah's. She blurted, "What I really want to say is—could you teach me to read like Priscilla does? Oh, I can read a receipt and all, when it comes to telling how much flour to put in a cake. And I can count the egg money but—"

Sarah beamed. "I'd be delighted to teach you, Mary."

Mary exuded enthusiasm, "I could pay you back in dresses and—'course you wouldn't have use for my services as a midwife, you being a single lady and all—"

Sarah almost blushed.

Mary's forehead suddenly creased. "It has to be a secret. You mustn't tell anybody, because of Henry, my husband. He thinks it's foolishness for women to learn anything. He says they don't need it. He's not home most of the time. He travels around breaking horses for folks. But when he is—any little thing upsets him. I just couldn't take a chance. You know what I mean?"

Sarah assured her, "Don't worry, Mary. The secret is ours. I'd be happy to teach you. And I could use some new dresses."

Sarah and Mary walked to the gate. After Mary left Sarah stood for a moment in the chilly air.

She had made a friend. She would begin with Mary.

Chapter Thirty One
THE DESERTION

Jaw set, hat pulled low, the man on the big bay gelding paused beside a creek. He dismounted and filled his leather canteen. His eyes clouded with inner anguish as he watched golden Aspen leaves drift from a tree on the creek bank and spin in the swift water. Then, horse and rider turned toward a rocky hillside. The horse's hooves rang out in the still air.

The man rode on, past town and trading post, past Indian hut and settler's shack. He asked nothing. He received nothing.

Hours later he reined in before a one-room schoolhouse and hollered, "I've come to get the boy."

A slight figure in a blue dress stood framed in the open doorway. Her hair glinted in the pale light. "Jake," she said faintly.

He saw her tremble. He restrained his impulse to run and hug her. He longed to bask in her sweetness, to tell her he missed her something fierce.

Instead, he spoke harshly, feigning indifference. "Are you gonna fetch the boy, Mrs. Weatherby?"

"Don't take him, Jake."

Why'd she have to murmur like this? It just made it harder for him. "What do you mean, 'don't'? It's time I started makin' a man out of him."

He noticed Sarah's eyes shimmer emerald green. That always meant tears were gathering.

Jake threw the reins over the pommel of his saddle and dismounted. "I'm wastin' time, Sarah." He strode toward her, his face hardened.

She spoke again, quietly. "How'd you know where to find us?"

He shrugged. "Didn't really plan on it. Went to the railroad depot at Three Corners to pick up the new window. Real glass don't come as easy as oiled paper, you know."

She winced.

"I was standin' there and just happened to look across the street. Saw Lady and the buggy. Right where you left 'em. Stable owner was hagglin' with a buyer so..." He let the sentence dangle and tried not to look at the softness of her cheek.

"Y-yes? Did he buy them? Do you know what happened to them?"

"I might."

"And you asked the stable man if I—if we—"

"Didn't need to ask. Stage only follows one road," he answered sharply.

"Are—are they still looking for me?"

"Who?"

"The sheriff—the law."

"Don't know. That's their lookout, not mine." He frowned. "You gonna fetch the boy? I'm waitin'."

He watched her chin tilt. Her familiar mannerism tugged hard at his emotions. He swallowed and looked away.

The children crowded around Sarah, craning their necks for a glimpse of the stranger. From inside the room came the shuffle of uneven footsteps. Like fluttering birds the children made way for Andy. He joined his mother in coat and hat.

"Pa! Pa!" His voice broke into a joyous cry. He hugged Jake around the waist and burrowed his face in the leather jerkin. "Can I go with you, Pa?" he said, his words muffled against Jake's chest.

Jake saw Sarah's struggle. She bit her lip to keep from crying. He dared not meet her eyes. Andy's hand slipped into his. "Pa needs me, Ma."

Jake lifted Andy onto the horse and tipped his hat, a sort of mocking gesture. The horse turned and started toward home. The first few miles were the hardest. Jake couldn't get the dust out of his eyes. Wasn't that the reason tears kept running down his cheeks?

Sarah watched the trail until she could no longer distinguish the small figure bobbing behind Jake's broad back. Her fists curled at her skirts. Tears streaked her cheeks and dropped from her chin.

"Teacher?"

Sarah looked down into a freckled face. "Yes, Priscilla?"

"Would you help me with my times tables?"

Sarah turned back into the room. "Of course, dear." She managed a watery smile. Beneath the pleasant teacher's face a fire raged.

School was dismissed and the children had gone. The waning sun slanted across Sarah's desk. Her gaze wandered restlessly over the water bucket in the corner and the big black stove with its endless appetite for wood. Could she go on without Andy? Could she return to her dreary cottage in Tanner Flats alone?

Something had broken inside her. She was seized with a pervading lethargy. The sight of Jake had sent a bolt through her chest. She wondered if he noticed how she trembled? It had taken all her strength to keep from running and throwing her arms around him. He must never know. It was obvious he hadn't missed her at all.

And when she refused to call Andy, he had said, "Are you gonna fetch him? I'm waitin'." Jake waiting? A smile quirked her mouth. Jake never waited for anybody. She always had to skip a little to keep up when they were walking. Remembering brought grief close to the surface. She buried her face in her hands.

"Miz Weatherby? Ma'am?"

Sarah jumped. "Oh, Hattie! I didn't hear you."

Hattie Barnes entered the schoolhouse timidly. Nervous fingers plucked at her purse strings. "We was wonderin'—the other ladies and me—"

Hattie had trouble focusing on Sarah's face. Her eyes shifted. One foot wiggled compulsively behind her long skirts.

"What is it, Hattie?" Sarah prompted.

Hattie's cheeks pinked. Her words, like a broken string of beads, rolled out in a tumble. "We'd like to use the school-house tomorrow, bein's it's Saturday, for our quiltin' bee. We figured we could move the benches and set up two frames 'stead of one, there bein' room."

As she spoke Hattie backed toward the door until she reached the threshold. Her face was puckered with some inner anxiety.

"Of course, Hattie. I don't mind. You know you don't have to ask. Is something bothering—?"

But Hattie was already on the schoolhouse steps. She called to Sarah, "Much obliged, Miz Weatherby."

Sarah watched Hattie run down the path. Puzzled, she snatched the broom. As she swept a sudden thought grew into a suspicion.

Chapter Thirty Two
THE DISMISSAL

Sarah's suspicion was confirmed at seven o'clock the next morning. Three school board members entered her kitchen and stood in a row.

Mr. McCary spoke first. "We have come to discuss a matter of grave importance. You have deceived us MRS. Weatherby."

Clarence Barnes recited his part in nasal tones, "Hattie seen the boy was gone. Just like the little ones said when they come home."

Emil Swenson twirled his hat with red-knuckled hands. "We don't want no trouble, ma'am. But you know the rules on married teachers. And that was yer husband who came and got yer son. Warn't no nephew a'tall."

Sarah looked from one to the other. No wonder Hattie had been nervous. They had sent her to spy. "I see," she said.

Swenson searched for a place to spit, found none and gulped. His adam's apple bobbed. "It ain't just the fact that you deceived us, ma'am. There's this other thing."

The tally of Sarah's sins traveled back along the line to Clarence Barnes. "You been tellin' the little girls when they grow up they kin vote, just like the menfolks."

McCary took it up, "We can't have our younguns talked to that way, Mrs. Weatherby. It's against the Good Book. If God Almighty wanted women to vote he would have said so."

"That's right," Clarence added, taking his turn.

Emil Swenson said, "We think you came here to stir up trouble. Just like—like—what's her name?"

Clarence elbowed Emil's ribs. "Abigail Duniway," he whispered.

"Yeah." Swenson's hat twirled faster. "Spreadin' haira—haira—"

"Heresy," McCary said impatiently.

"That's the word." Swenson pounced on it. "Harassy."

Sarah masked her agitation. "So you are relieving me of my position?"

Swenson and Barnes cast sheepish glances at each other. Sarah knew they expected tears, perhaps pleading. What they witnessed instead was a woman poised and controlled—just barely.

McCary added the final touch. "We are closing the school, Mrs. Weatherby. We have no choice."

Swenson moved toward the door. "Beg pardon, ma'am. Clarence and me got business elsewhere." The two men shuffled out.

McCary lingered, his beady eyes assessing her. Sarah noticed something shiny in his palm.

"I am returning next month's rent to you, Mrs. Weatherby. As you know, Washington Territory will become a state next year. My cousin has expressed a wish to settle here. I feel it is my Christian duty to provide him with a home. This home. I'm sure you understand."

Sarah bit her lip. Her reply was scissor-clipped. "I understand a great deal more than you think I do, Mr. McCary. Her fingernails dug into her palms. "Would you please excuse me now. I have work to do."

McCary bowed over his stomach and tiptoed out. Sarah grabbed the teakettle, flung the door wide and poured the boiling water on the path. The steam rolled toward McCary, billowing around his fast-pumping spindly legs.

Two hours later Sarah buckled her portmanteau and turned slowly in the dismal little house.

"Well, Mr. McCary," she said to the silent walls, "your cousin is welcome to it." But where would she go? There didn't seem to be a place on this earth that wanted her. She was desperately alone.

She carried the valise outside, left the key on a hook by the door and started down the boardwalk.

A dove called. At least, she thought it was a dove.

"Yoo-hoo," it mourned. "Yoo-hoo," again.

Sarah turned. Mary Applegate fluttered a white hand-kerchief between the withered vines covering her front porch. She called again, dove-mellow, "Yoo-hoo."

Sarah hurried up Mary's porch steps. "I have to say goodbye, Mary. The school board has dismissed me."

Mary drew her inside. "Yes, I know. But you don't have to leave."

Sarah set down her heavy portmanteau and rubbed her aching arm. "But they said—"

Mary took a firm stance. "I know what they said. Gossip travels faster than the ague. But you don't have to leave. Not unless you want to."

Puzzled, Sarah waited and Mary rushed on. "Those silly men are so self-righteous with their rules and commandments. But their wives are right proud of the way the younguns are learning. And I don't want to lose you. Not when I'm beginning to read Priscilla's primers. Stay, Sarah."

She put her hand on Sarah's arm. "Stay with me. Please. We can have school right here in my house. Henry's not home most of the time anyway. And when he does come— if he kicks up a fuss—Well, to tell the truth, I'm getting tired of his bullying ways. Maybe one of these days I'll just tell him to stay away. This is my house. My pa willed it to me."

Her eyes twinkled. "If you'll stay I can guarantee a lot of younguns will find some excuse to visit Priscilla every day." She giggled, enjoying the joke.

Sarah noted the sincerity in Mary's face. Mary truly wanted her. And if the other children came—she could teach them. The only one missing would be Andy, dear Andy...

"I don't know, Mary. Should I?"

Mary decided for her. "Yes, you should. We want you. We need you. Now come to the kitchen and let's have a cup of tea while I show you a new bustle pattern."

Mary guessed right. In the days that followed boys and

girls crowded around her kitchen table, their eager faces turned toward Sarah. Primers, maps and wall charts from the school-house began to appear. When Sarah asked, "How did you get these?" Mary only winked and smiled.

Every morning ice skimmed the water bucket. Flocks of Canadian geese honked overhead on their way to southern feeding grounds. Week after week the thermometer signaled the approach of winter.

At four o'clock on a Thursday afternoon Priscilla left to spend the night with a friend. As the clock chimed five the local boot maker burst through the door.

"Come quick, Mary. Sadie's started the birthin' and she's awful uncomfortable."

Mary, the midwife, gathered her bag of herbal palliatives. At the door, she gasped, "Oh! Henry's wagon is turning the corner. Why did he choose tonight to come home? He'll be angry if food's not on the table."

She fidgeted nervously with her hat pin, jabbing it repeatedly through the felt into the bun atop her head. "Sarah, dear, if you don't mind, just find something in the pantry for his supper." She whisked out the door mumbling, "...wouldn't you know it."

Sarah tied her apron strings while a thread of apprehension quivered in her chest. As she opened the pantry door she heard Henry's boots scrape across the porch.

An hour later the only sounds in the kitchen were the ticking clock and the occasional crack and hiss of wood in the cookstove.

Sarah wondered if Henry could hear her swallow. When she poured him a second cup of coffee and passed the cream, his roughened fingertips brushed her hand. His touch sent an unpleasant shudder down her spine.

At last Henry pushed back his chair. Sarah emptied the teakettle's scalding water into a dishpan and tempered it with cold from the bucket. As she slivered a bar of Mary's home-made lye soap into the water, she heard Henry moving around in his bedroom.

Suddenly he was behind her holding a kerosene lamp. "Mrs. Weatherby."

Startled, Sarah clattered a cup in the dishpan. "Yes, Mr. Applegate?"

"Would you mind coming in here a minute?"

Something in his eyes made a muscle tense in her stomach. She hesitated, then dried her hands and reluctantly followed him into the bedroom.

"I've lost a button on the carpet," he said.

"Where did you drop it, Mr. Applegate?" she asked, chiding herself for raising a flag of distrust in her mind.

"Over here somewhere." He set the lamp on the dresser and got down on his hands and knees. "Now, I figure if we both look close we'll come up with the button."

Sarah knelt, her fingers passing lightly over the carpet. The lamp flickered. Henry worked his way around until he was between Sarah and the door. He kicked the door shut and stood up.

"Found it!"

Shocked, Sarah rose slowly. She stared at him.

Henry's eyes glowed in the lamplight. "Just you and me, Mrs. Weatherby. We're alone now."

"You're making a dreadful mistake, Mr. Applegate. Let me out of here at once."

He advanced step by step, leering at her. "No. No mistake. I've been watching you. Didn't know that, did you?" His laugh was a dry humorless cackle. "I figured you out a long time ago."

Panic pulsed at Sarah's throat. *His eyes, like hog's eyes...an image blurred by time...the day she fed Big Lil's hogs, a shaded place, a girl...*

"You!" Sarah cried. "Now I remember. Under the willow tree—It was you. You with Salvia Ruehl."

"Yes, Mrs. Weatherby. I was there. And you, respectable surveyor's wife, hurrying by with your clothes under your arm. Didn't want folks to see you. Didn't want—"

"No, no, you're wrong—"

"Didn't know I had you figured out. You thought nobody'd—"

"You're wrong. You're wrong!" she screamed. "Let me out of here."

"Salvia was just a game, but you're—"

"You used that poor girl. Then you threw her away like a dirty rag—like a dirty rag—" Sarah's voice ended in a sob.

Applegate's shadow leaped on the wall.

Sarah bumped into the dresser. "You destroyed Salvia. You killed her!"

Sudden anger cut furrows in his face. "You shouldn't talk to me like that. She was just a simple-minded girl. What difference does it make?" His expression changed. His face sagged. "But you're a woman—here with me—just the two of us and nobody to know."

Sarah searched frantically behind her on the dresser. Her fingertips grazed a hairbrush, a box of dusting powder, the lamp...

One step closer and...he reached for her. Sarah gripped the lamp, brought it around and dashed it into his face.

Applegate shrieked and fell to the floor in a shower of flame and shattered glass. He writhed on the carpet, flailing and kicking.

Sarah stumbled over him. "Help! Help!" she cried in a broken voice. She pulled and yanked at the knob. At last she wrenched open the door. She staggered through the kitchen, onto the porch and plunged into the night.

Her legs carried her past houses with lighted windows, past woodpiles and snow-covered compost heaps. She crashed through a dried corn patch. Dogs barked. She heard a mother's voice call children home to hearthside. Aromas of suppers cooking filled the air. Still she ran.

At the edge of town she collapsed beneath a tree. She lay trembling in the damp pine needles while silent tears soothed and washed her wounded spirit.

Sarah stood. She shook violently. Her teeth chattered. She wandered away from the tree and chanced upon a wagon track. The faint lines of the ruts led to a shed beside the road.

Sarah approached it cautiously. She groped for the door latch and eased it open. Moonlight filtered through a cob-webbed window, revealing tools propped against the walls and bundles of gunny sacks tied with twine. An over-flowing grain bin loomed in a corner.

She bumped against a square-bladed shovel. It clanged to the floor, the echo ringing in the silence.

"If I could just lie down for a while," she murmured. "If I could get warm..."

With numb fingers she opened a bundle of sacks and spread them on the floor. A wool fleece lay folded on a shelf. She carried it to her sack bed and covered herself.

Curled under the smelly fleece, Sarah stared into the darkness. She was bereft of husband and child and cast out. Had God abandoned her as well? Exhaustion drew her mind into a grey fuzzy repose and she slept.

Chapter Thirty Four
THE DESPERATE DEED

A squeaking wagon wheel awakened Sarah. She sat up. It was morning. Voices and the steady clop clop of teams pulling wagons drew her to the dirty window. She saw two men standing in the road. Their steamy breath hung in the chill air before their faces as they laughed and talked.

"Gonna be some contest, by Jove. That Danny Millthatch can fell trees almost as good as his Pa."

"Well, he ought to. He's as big as a ox. Who's he up against?"

"Some boy name of Weatherby. His pa brought him down from the high country braggin' on how strong he is."

"Weatherby? Ain't that the name of that teacher they run off a couple months ago?"

"Yup. Only some say she holed up somewhere. Still hangin' around town. I never seen her though. Kinda queer, that one. Folks said she sounded like a preacher when it come to women's rights and such. Kinda glad they threw her out. No tellin' how she'd a poisoned the younguns minds."

"S'pose this Weatherby kid's her boy? I heard she was teachin' under false pretenses, married and all."

"Could be. Hey, you placin' bets?"

"Yup."

"Count me in."

The men strolled out of sight toward Tanner Flats. Sarah hugged herself and shivered. She saw more people, a parade of buggies, horseback riders, couples striding along and children skipping. All laughing and talking, they were planning to watch that Weatherby kid get trounced.

Sarah uttered an anguished cry. A tree felling contest...the Weatherby boy...his pa bragging...what had Jake done? Hadn't he any sense at all?

She had to go back. There was no alternative. She

would stop the contest if she had to throw herself in front of the axes.

The volume of travelers thinned. Sarah watched a few stragglers hurry past. She draped a gunny sack over her shoulders and crept out of the shed.

She was suddenly conscious of her appearance. In her wild flight from Henry Applegate her hair pins had come undone and now lay scattered somewhere along the wagon track. Her blonde curls framed her face and fell to her shoulders in waves. Bits of sheep fleece clung to her skirts. And the smudge on her cheek matched the film of grain dust that covered her clothes. She shook her skirts and tried to smooth her hair.

A spotted dog caught up with her. He wagged his tail and loped alongside. She reached down to pet him. He gave her a sideways glance, tongue lolling, then trotted off.

"Even the dog deserts me," she muttered. Her breath flowed raggedly over the lump in her throat.

Far ahead the crowd still moved toward town. As Sarah rounded a bend she saw a clearing, two tall pines in its center. Tiny figures moved. Was one of them Andy? Something glinted, reflecting the morning light. Sarah knew it was the blade of an axe.

She hurried, clutching the scratchy sack to her throat. Reaching the circle of spectators, she pressed into their midst. "Please let me through. Excuse me. Would you move aside? Please, I need to get through."

Her polite inquiries were ignored. Shoulder to shoulder, bib overall to calico skirt, they formed an impenetrable wall.

"Don't push, lady."

"Quit shovin'."

"I was here first."

Sarah pleaded, "But you don't understand. I must stop this contest. They can't—"

The ring of the axes resounded. Sarah heard their echo in the forest beyond. It was too late. She bent her head. "Oh dear God, no. I'm too late. My son."

Her eyes filled and spilled over. She covered her dirty cheeks with her hands. Each strike of an axe was like a blow to her body. Her shoulders sagged. She stood, shivering and dejected, waiting for the inevitable humiliation.

Presently the spectator's comments penetrated her dark thoughts.

"Look at that Weatherby kid swing."

"That youngun's sure got muscles for his age."

"Say now, this's gettin' lively. Maybe I bet on the wrong boy."

Muscles? On Andy? Sarah's head snapped up. Desperate hope crowded the heels of her despair. She flexed her elbows and pushed further toward the front. There was Andy's blonde head and his lean back. A surge of love swept through her.

Andy's axe bit into the tree with steady, measured blows. He braced with his bad leg and led with the good one. Sarah's mouth opened slightly in amazement. She saw the muscles ripple under his shirt. There was strength in his body and determination on his face. And directly across the circle she glimpsed Jake, grinning with pride.

Sarah's eyes slanted momentarily toward the Millthatch boy. He seemed awkward. He was tiring. Sweat dribbled down his flabby face.

A current of excitement raced through the crowd. They jostled one another. Someone started to clap and chant. The crowd took it up. Mr. McCary hopped into the center of the circle and cocked his head at each boy. He checked his watch. He raised his hand. Both trees swayed ominously. The crowd grew silent.

Andy's tree hissed, popped and crashed to the ground.

McCary's arm cut a sharp swath through the air. He sang out, "The winner—is—Andy Weatherby!"

A roar of cheering erupted around Sarah. People slapped one another on the back and danced in circles.

Sarah started forward, tears streaming down her cheeks.

"Andy. Andy," she called.

People pressed on all sides. They elbowed her back and stepped in front of her.

"Please let me through. That's my boy. I need to—"

Rough hands pushed at her. "Sure, lady, sure. Wait your turn like everybody else."

Hysteria rose in Sarah's throat. She couldn't breathe. She was drowning in a sea of people. What if Andy and Jake should leave before she reached them? What if they hadn't seen her?

Suddenly a man sprang from the crowd. He blocked her path. Sarah looked up into the glowering face of Henry Applegate. His arm shot out. His finger wagged.

"That's the one. The harlot. The Weatherby woman. A common slut."

"Wha-what?" Sarah's mind whirled dizzily. Her stomach turned at the sight of the fiery burns on his face.

The people stared, stunned and hushed by his accusation. Then Sarah watched in horror as they surged forward. Their backs created a wall, shutting her off from the center of the clearing. Their voices rose once more in noisy celebration.

The world stood still and she was alone again with Henry Applegate.

Chapter Thirty Five
THE DESTINY

Vengeance darkened Applegate's face. He whispered coarsely, "Just you and me alone again, Mrs. Weatherby. This time you won't get away. You're gonna wish you hadn't thrown that lamp."

"No," she murmured involuntarily. "No". She stepped backward. Damp tendrils of hair stuck to her cheeks. Her eyes widened in fear.

Applegate moistened his lips with a darting tongue. "You can't escape. Nobody will help you. They don't care what happens to you."

He inched toward her.

"No, please, no."

His arm was extended. Claw-like fingers reached for her. She envisioned them drawing blood and tearing flesh. His papery laugh scratched the air. "I'll teach you not to throw lamps at me." He gripped her arm. She stumbled away from his grasp, ripping the fabric of her sleeve. Behind her, the crowd's joyous celebration became a mocking counterpoint to Applegate's invective.

She must find a place to hide. She must run away. Whirling, she spied the dark woods beyond the clearing, lifted her skirts and raced toward the sheltering trees.

Her feet slipped on pine needles. Branches caught at her clothes. The gunny sack tore from her shoulders, fastened to a bramble bush and flapped feebly.

And then she fell hard, flat on her face. A broken coal shovel protruded from under her skirts. She had tripped on it. Beneath her the ground vibrated with Applegate's heavy tread as he slashed through the brush searching for her.

In her terror faces and images flashed through her mind: Judge Featherstone, Phil LeCour, Henry Applegate, and yes, even Jake, dear Jake—she had run from them all. There was no safety in running. She knew that now. She would run no further.

Her fingers closed over the weathered handle of the coal shovel. She struggled to her knees. A sense of resolve helped her on her feet. God had given her an indomitable spirit. It was a fire in her soul that would not be quenched.

She must stand, stand alone if need be, no matter what happened. It was the only way she could be true to God and to herself.

She gripped the shovel handle, holding the rusted blade high over her shoulder. Behind her the branches of a tree spread wide as if to shield her.

"This is my witness tree," she said, with her chin held high. "My witness tree. I will not run another step."

One heartbeat. Two. Henry Applegate burst through the bushes. His contorted features bore down on her.

She struck.

The crack echoed through the woods. Applegate's face crumpled like wadded paper. He fell at her feet. The fingers of his one hand, still extended, brushed against the hem of her skirt. Sarah shuddered and twisted to avoid their touch.

She dropped the shovel. It was over. But there was no triumph in it. No triumph at all. Where would she go now? What would she do? She clung to the tree, panting and nauseated.

The tramping of approaching feet and the murmur of voices turned her head.

"Lookit that. She kilt him."

"Naw, he'll come to."

"I say she kilt him."

The crowd surrounded her, peering into her face with malevolent stares. Some held sticks. Others fingered rocks.

"She's a murderer."

"Let's take her."

Over their heads an authoritative voice rang out. "Stand back. Stand back, I say."

An electric tingle shot through Sarah. She felt the rough texture of Jake's coat as his arms encircled and supported her. He whispered in her hair, "Dad gum it, you're sure a hard woman to catch up to."

He raised his voice again, "Go home, all of you. Tend to your own business." He pointed to Applegate, now moaning and trying to sit up. "And take this varmint with you."

Sarah sagged against Jake. Familiar emotions swept her body. Love for Jake. Her love had never waned.

Jake led her toward the clearing. Andy ran to meet them, balancing a new axe in his hand.

"Ma. Ma. Look at my prize. I won, Ma. I won."

Sarah rushed forward and hugged him. "Andy. My boy. Oh, how I've missed you."

"Ma, did you see me fell the tree? Did you see it?"

"Yes, Son, I watched you. I'm so proud of you. You've—"She stopped. She questioned Jake with her eyes. "You knew, didn't you?" she said softly. "You knew Andy could be strong. And you gave him the chance to know it for himself."

She saw Ralphie coming toward them, leading a pony. He said "Jake bought her for me. Isn't she a beaut?" Then shyly, "Sure wish you'd come home, Mrs. Weatherby. I'm awful tired of eatin' Jake's beans."

Sarah and Jake boarded the buggy. Andy and Ralphie followed on Moses and the new pony.

With a warm brick at her feet and a blanket tucked around her Sarah asked, "How did you get Lady back?"

Jake smiled. "Thought you'd catch on that day at the school-house. I wasn't goin' to let some stranger take Lady and maybe mistreat her, so I stepped up and outbid him."

The buggy jiggled and swayed as Lady settled into an easy trot toward home.

Jake said, "Abigail Duniway was in town last month."

"Abigail? Wish I'd been there."

Jake reached around Sarah and drew her close. "She gave a speech in front of the town hall. Nobody booed either. She said she was glad there was one woman with enough spunk to work for women's suffrage no matter what. She was talkin' about you, I reckon. She's comin' back in the spring when the roads dry up."

Sarah clapped her hands together. "I want to be there. I WILL be there. And—"

She sat up abruptly. The blanket slipped from her shoulders. "But, I can't, Jake. Stop the buggy. We can't go on. I can't go home. There's Judge Featherstone and—and—why did I ever think things could work out? It's no use. It's no use." Sobbing, she fell against Jake.

Jake pulled on the reins. "Whoa, Lady. Whoa, girl." He gently lifted Sarah and tilted her face toward him. "You think I'd come so far in this bone-jarring contraption if you couldn't go home?"

"But, I can't. I can't. He—he said—jail, that's where he'll put me—in jail."

Jake tucked the blanket around her again. He flicked the reins over Lady's back and they started on. "Don't you hear any news at all in this rabbit warren of a town? Judge Featherstone's dead, Sarah. Right after the trial somebody stabbed him."

"Stabbed? How awful."

"Some folks thought you did it."

"They thought I—? Oh, Jake."

"I told 'em they'd better get shut of that idea fast. New circuit judge looked at your file. Said it was a bunch of nonsense. Threw it out. Said he didn't have time for such foolishness."

Sarah began to relax. "You mean I'm free? Really free? Then I could have gone home before, except..." She gazed at his face wistfully, "...I didn't think you wanted me, Jake."

"Didn't think I wanted you?" Jake looked startled. "Where'd you get that idea? If I hadn't found you, Sarah, I'd have gone on lookin' for the rest of my life. I love you. Don't you know that? Guess I never told you often enough."

Sarah snuggled close. Weariness was overtaking her. She struggled to keep her eyes open.

"Want some more news," Jake asked.

"Yes. It's so good to hear your voice." The words came slowly. Her head rested on Jake's shoulder.

"The way I see it, land's gonna be all settled one of these days. Surveyin's comin' to a close. Thought maybe I'd run for the State Legislature. Need a strong woman beside me to do that. Somebody to support me when I make speeches in favor of women's suffrage."

He glanced at Sarah's face. Her eyes were closed.

"You see, I kinda changed my mind on that subject. The way Abigail Duniway sees it, things are gonna change. Nugget's changin' already. You wouldn't know the town, Sarah. Got us a detective now. Not much for looks. A little hunchback. Say's he's had lots of practice spyin' on folks."

"I was settin' in front of the mercantile the other day. He came along and kicked the buggy wheel. Muttered somethin' to himself. It sounded like 'looks just the same'. What do you suppose he was talkin' about?" Jake turned to Sarah for a response but she was asleep. He kissed her lightly. "Yep. Senator and Mrs. Weatherby. Kind of a pretty ring to it."